MICHAEL DOUGLAS

and the Douglas Clan

MICHAEL DOUGLAS

and the Douglas Clan

Annene Kaye & Jim Sclavunos

W H ALLEN · LONDON
1989

First published in the United States of America by Paperjacks Ltd,
Toronto and New York, 1989

Set in Baskerville by Input Typesetting Ltd, London
Printed and bound in Great Britain by
Mackays of Chatham PLC, Chatham, Kent
for the Publishers, W H Allen & Co Plc
Sekforde House, 175/9 St. John Street, London EC1V 4LL

ISBN 0 491 03219 6

CONTENTS

For Martha and Herbert Kaye,
and Genevieve Sclavunos.

Thanks to: Cathy Ruszkowski, the waitress at Jolanta's, Claire Lawrence-Slater, Nick Gillespie, Truus De Groot, 2M, Jim Connor, and the guy in the xerox room at Lincoln Center.

INTRODUCTION

'At Hollywood's annual Oscar ceremony, in front of millions of TV viewers around the world, Kirk Douglas put his arm around his actor/producer son Michael, and said: "If I'd known he was going to be so successful, I'd have been nicer to him as a kid." '

– Ivor Davis in *Company* magazine, December 1985

Michael Douglas is a man of contradictions. He appears casual – tousled hair, polo shirts, comfortable suits . . . the polar opposite of the 'Gorden Gekko' power look he wore like armour in *Wall Street*. But this guy plays in the big leagues, the *really* big leagues. When looking at pictures of this friendly, mild-mannered individual it's hard to imagine that he's probably got a bank account total which resembles a long-distance phone number. This is a man who stopped talking about how much money he made in 1975, when *One Flew Over the Cuckoo's Nest* began hurdling towards the $20,000,000 mark it ultimately surpassed in 1987. This is a man who probably never regretted bypassing the possible mass-merchandising of *Romancing the Stone* and *The Jewel of the Nile*; the inherent silliness of little plastic 'Jack Colton' dolls must be easier to avoid when the profits from the two films exceed $450,000,000. Not that all of this money finds its way into Michael's pocket – he's only the producer and star – but suffice it to say that Michael Douglas, despite his easygoing looks, is a very rich man and consequently a very powerful man.

Michael Douglas appears to shift and slide, true to the chameleon characteristics he has attributed to himself. Although he's gained a stronger identity as he's continued to rack up brownie points in the star system, he still carries an aura of his old self, whatever that was, and it was whatever other people wanted him to be according to Michael. Herein lies another contradiction – a coexistent stability and insecurity, the vaguest hint that this VIP can't quite visualise himself in those terms. Though well on his way to resolving any lingering doubts, he manages to impart a slight hesitancy by his tone, body language, and eyes which most celebrities strive to conceal. Quite simply, this hint of vulnerability is one key to his public appeal. Women like it. Men like it. It allowed him to paint a sympathetic portrait of an initially unlikeable character, the schmuck who cheated on his wife with (out of all the women in the world) a potentially homicidal, rabbit-boiling lunatic. When reduced to these terms, it's difficult to believe that millions of people who rushed to theatres, creating the box-office blockbuster of the year, actually felt sorry for *Fatal Attraction*'s Dan Gallagher. Producers Sherry Lansing and Stanley Jaffe were right on the money when they decided that Douglas is perhaps the only actor around with the ability to pull off *that* trick.

Many contradictions create Michael Douglas's particular persona – common and uncommon ones. Michael is a man who can be in front of the camera one minute and behind it the next, but admits to some discomfort when trying to balance his family life and his business life. He grew up on both the east coast and the west, adapting to the tribal rights of each. He's an entrepreneur with a 'hippie' mentality. And, most importantly, Michael Douglas is a man seemingly intensely influenced by his famous father, but also apparently in turmoil over his role as 'son of a superstar'.

Because of his parents' divorce, Michael and his brother Joel were bicoastal kids who clung together to try to keep everything in perspective, shuttling between their mom and stepdad's relatively normal life in Connecticut and their father and stepmom and two half brothers' glamorous existence in California. 'I would cry on the plane going west and I would cry going east,' Joel says. But unlike Mom, Dad was always there; in magazines and on screens, bigger than life. And in the end, it seems that Michael and his brothers have been partially affected by Kirk the human being, and Kirk the macho movie star.

'He was tough, really tough. I think ultimately that toughness has been a benefit to all his sons, although it was a real close call,' Michael explains. 'Some of that quality that was larger than life on the screen – that presence, that anger – carried over into his own life. We were in awe of his anger.' Kirk's anger sprung from his rough past as Issur Danielovitch, the child of immigrants who overcame every obstacle, including his own father's desertion. 'I am always fighting. I am reliving the Danielovitch story,' Kirk says. His four sons never knew Issur Danielovitch, but they seem to equate him with some of the people their father portrayed on screen. One of Michael's most enigmatic contradictions is apparent acceptance of his father as the heroic creature he played in the movies. Granted, the fact that Michael and Joel didn't live with Kirk all the time might have added to his mystique, but the two spent time with their dad on location, watching him fabricate these beings. Then they went home with him and watched him do normal, fatherly things. Yet they both ran screaming from the theatre when Vincent Van Gogh/Daddy cut off his ear. Michael says, 'Kirk Douglas is certainly a hard act to follow. I mean, there he was hanging from the cross in *Spartacus*, walking across the ranks of oars in *The Vikings*. . .' At the same time he's been known to say, 'One of the good things about growing up in Hollywood is that you do get to see the industry as a business and you develop a sense of reality and perspective about it all. I saw my father and . . . friends, their successes and failures. I saw them living real lives, instead of reading the myths about them in the tabloids.' All this indicates a lack of resolution concerning his father and his world.

'I gave my sons some advice about the movie business,' Kirk told the *New York Post*. 'I told them to stay out of it. . . You see how much influence I have.' There's been an air of competition between Kirk and his sons since Michael's first rebellious stirrings as a somewhat confused post-adolescent who dropped out of college to work in a gas station. When Michael came out on top with *One Flew Over the Cuckoo's Nest*, his first production originating from a property Kirk had tried to sell for ten years, obviously the balance of the relationship changed significantly. Unfortunately, his parents' divorce and ensuing changes over the years had reportedly put their egos on unsteady ground to begin with. 'It was a question of the old stag versus the young stag,' says Diana Douglas, Michael's mother. Finally, a deal was struck, and according to Peter Douglas (a producer himself), 'Dad has made about $15 million on the picture so far, so whatever his feelings were, he has been well compensated.'

While telling his sons to stay away from acting and the movies, Kirk simultaneously provided jobs for them on the sets and exposure to the business of *the* business. Michael and Joel were still in their teens when they had a crack at menial movie labour, while in the distance Kirk loudly suggested that a lawyer is a fine thing to be. But in spite of this particular contradiction, Kirk passed on a solid dictum which all of his kids eventually lived up to, one way or another. Referring to Michael in 1973, he said his first son was a 'very talented actor, and he'll function. In my family that's the key word. All I ever said to my sons is function. . .' He later continued, 'What's that phrase, "Let there be spaces in their togetherness." All my kids are very independent. Many times when I'm around Michael, I am the father of Michael Douglas, rather than he is the son of Kirk Douglas.'

This independence extends beyond family matters. Kirk also taught his sons to remain somewhat independent of the main trunk of the movie business. Since the early 1970s, Michael's been involved in his own production companies and an increasingly dizzying array of deals with everyone from his father to the largest film companies. Joel does business with Michael and Peter, via a Mexican production company. Peter does business with Kirk, producing a movie and television specials which feature him. Michael has worked with corporations which Eric is doing business with, etc. etc. The family's business life remains slanted towards the family, big business with some of the helpful aspects of a small business mentality. The boys have made good use of the lessons their dad taught them (complete with detailed examples from his own life no doubt; Kirk gained a reputation for being 'difficult' early on). Kirk paved his way to stardom by doing things that people told him he shouldn't do – by forming his own companies and diversifying (a lot of Kirk's business is run by his second wife, Anne), and taking the parts he wanted . . . even if he had to break a contract to do it.

Michael's had to push to keep from getting swept away by the strength of his influence, but he managed, creating yet another dislocative factor in their lives. 'I had to keep a strong grip on them,' Diana explains. Michael and Joel would come home from vacation with Kirk and Anne throwing their clothes about, and when ordered to put them away, they replied that Dad had a butler to see to such things. Such crossovers weren't permitted.

In a pivotal dissection of the Douglas Dynasty in *Vanity Fair*, journalist Marie Brenner compared the Douglases to the Kennedy family, citing the sons' needs to compete with their fathers on home territory. She cited a time when Douglas senior golfed with Kennedy senior. During their conversation the actor sought the political maven's advice for raising a brood. Joe Kennedy said, 'Make your boys independent and then they will come back to you.' From the way things seem today, it appears that he did . . . and they did. The family is more and more tightly knit, and Michael is beginning to identify with his father, the man who inspired Anne Douglas to begin her excellent and revealing characterisation, entitled *My Awful Wedded Husband*, with the words, 'Living with my husband is like sitting in a beautiful garden right next to a volcano that may erupt at any moment.' The eldest Douglas son can now reflect, 'Think of it, here are people like my father and me who are getting paid to give all day long, to be charming and funny and sexy to the public. Reporters follow you around taking down your words. You get a false sense of importance. Then you go home and the kids won't listen to you and you wind up screaming your head off because you are not getting that same kind of attention.'

In any case, in 1988 it seemed that Michael Douglas firmly broke out of his father's shadow in at least one area when he won an Oscar for Best Actor, an honour which evaded Kirk three times. Michael Douglas is slowly and surely coming into his own in an impressively indisputable fashion. Perhaps one of the more indicative gestures were these words he had for his own son, Cameron: ‘I guess I’ll have to think about raising him to cope with the famous father syndrome.’ It may end up being a congenital symptom in the Douglas Clan. We should all function this well.

Chapter One

HUMBLE BEGINNINGS

'I've got two boys of my own and it's a pretty nice feeling for a father to look at his sons and know that they can become the happiest, most successful fellows in the world, because they're growing up in the land of opportunity.'

– Kirk Douglas, in an article entitled 'Here's What America Means to Me. . .'

'I'm the most disliked actor in Hollywood. No, not because I'm a perfectionist. Just because I'm me.'

– Kirk Douglas, June 30, 1964, *New York World Telegraph and Sun*

'He has always liked bowling. . . . He is an omnivorous eater.'

– Columnist Sidney Skolsky January 11, 1953

'I think a lot of what I've tried to accomplish in life was really an attempt to get a pat on the back from my father. But he wasn't a man who showed his feelings easily. When I asked him what he thought of me in a film he'd say, "Yeah, yeah." Yet his friends all told me, "Your father is so proud of you." He just couldn't say it.'

– Kirk Douglas, 1969

It's the fall of 1940. Kirk Douglas is up to his proverbial chin in his own particular brand of showbiz pathos . . . piece by piece he is constructing the perfect movie star. His tools are his style, wit, and guile. His building blocks are whatever he can grab, by hard work or bull-headed determination, plus anything fate throws in his lap. Mr Douglas is single-mindedly ploughing his way toward his destiny: superstar status, a multimillion dollar network of corporations, a house filled with Impressionist paintings, and a dynasty of his own – two wives and four sons who will be profoundly affected by his material and ethical legacy.

At this point, fate conspired to throw a girl in his lap. Kirk, a student at the American Academy of Dramatic Arts, is the willing recipient of an attractive classmate's adoration – hardly a newsworthy situation, it would seem, for a blond-haired, blue-eyed, bedimpled, macho young thespian to encounter. 'Kirk was my first big crush when I was fifteen,' the woman professed many years later. 'I was a wide-eyed baby, and he seemed an experienced man of the world.' Consider, however, that the fluttery teenager radiating all this palpitating adolescent puppy love is one Ms Lauren 'Betty' Bacall, and suddenly you're slapped in the face with the paintbrush which seems to colour most of Mr Kirk Douglas's life. Nothing ordinary will do . . . you have just entered The CinemaScope Zone.

The Academy itself was a long way from Movieland, geographically* and spiritually. Its students were taught the

*West Fifty-seventh Street, as a matter of fact, close to Carnegie Hall.

broad gestures of stage acting. The school provided areas for fencing, dancing, and stuntwork, small stages for rehearsals, and specially lit rooms where 'the kids' mastered the intricacies of plastering their faces with orange pancake makeup. The demands were strenuous; the Academy's skilled staff rigorously drilled its pupils physically and mentally.

Ms Bacall, along with the other pupils, spent her days exercising her talents in various ways – yelling and making faces (voice projection exercises) and mimicking everything from teapots to squirrels (either humiliation or interpretation exercises). In between these acrobatics and histrionics, she attended the senior class's weekly performances, staged in the Carnegie Lyceum every Friday evening. Although a certain someone immediately caught her eye, it took time for her to catch his.

'One Friday night, at intermission, I was on the landing chatting with friends when I glanced down the stairs and there he was, looking at me – my hero, the marvellous actor . . . Kirk Douglas,' recalls Bacall in her autobiography *By Myself.* 'Of course I started to tremble. All my life, at any emotional time, I have trembled.'

Prevailing winds at the Academy were casual and friendly; Ms Bacall found striking up a conversation a simple matter: 'We talked. Briefly and casually – and then . . . more and more easily. He finally invited me to a Chinese restaurant in Greenwich Village. He told me all about himself. He had no money at all. Once he spent a night in jail because he had no place to sleep. The drama of that – and the effect it had on one as impressionable as I! "Oh, how he has suffered!" I thought. He really had struggled.'

By the time these two collided on their respective roads to glory, Kirk Douglas had spent most of his quarter century on earth fighting, clawing, and battling his way through every obstacle lodged in his path. He personifies the classic Hollywood rags-to-riches fable, and despite its Discovered-in-a-Drugstore overtones, the rough times and traumas Kirk faced in his early years were a reality. They endowed him with an intense craving for success; he derived much of his strength from those bad times, which haunted him even after he'd attained his goals. In spite of this, Mr Douglas is the first to admit, 'Life is like a B-picture script . . . it's that corny. If I had my life story offered to me to film, I'd turn it down.'

However, the effects of this B movie on the Douglas Clan were of epic proportions. Unlike most kids, Michael, Joel, Peter, and Eric could read about their father's accomplishments in the fanzines, and so could everyone around them. Kirk Douglas gave his children many gifts, but with them came the burden of a rather large pair of footsteps to follow in.

Kirk was born Issur Danielovitch on December 9, 1916, in Amsterdam, New York. His parents, Herschel and Bryna, were recent immigrants who fled the poverty, chaos, and fervent anti-Semitism of Mother Russia circa 1910. They arrived at Ellis Island with their dreams bolstered by those oft-cited fables of the good life awaiting them in the United States. Herschel, illiterate and unskilled, was determined to use his strong back and powerful physique to provide a basic living for his family . . . if not something more substantial. 'They were simple peasant people,' Kirk wrote of his parents in his quaint patriotic diatribe, 'Here's What America Means to Me.' 'They arrived here with their hearts full of dreams. They heard that the streets were paved with gold and they believed it.

'It wasn't too long ago that my mother told me that she had found something better than gold bricks in the United States. She found freedom and a country where she and my father could raise a family of seven children and each one of them was able to get an education and to choose a way of life. Who wouldn't agree with my mother? *Freedom is better than gold bricks.*'

Back in the real world of oppressive poverty, Kirk's mom would have probably blessed the appearance of even a *little* gold brick. The Danielovitchs, to put it mildly, didn't have a pot to piss in; but at least no pogroms rampaged through the streets of upstate New York.

'There were nine of us in the family, and we were poor,' Kirk recounts. 'Lots of times we didn't have enough to eat.' At other times, he waxes a bit more rhapsodically, 'My family lived intimately with hunger' or with a touch of sarcasm: 'We lived in a charming place in the high rent district – above a garage and near the slaughterhouse. Nobody was able to get spoiled in our family.'

Years later, wife Anne would tease, '. . . the only thing that ever would destroy my husband would be to find anybody as poor as he says he was. There *are* some, but in his mind he was the poorest, most miserable child that ever lived.' Realistically, the Danielovitchs' financial situation was tough, but not impossible. 'We ate all right most of the time; our clothes were not exactly the height of style, but we didn't really suffer. A lot of people were in the same shape about that time – during the depression years. We all went to work as soon as we were able.'

Amsterdam's employment opportunities were as multi-dimensional as they were fascinating; one could work in either the Mohawk or Sanford mills, if one's lineage conformed to the expected religious and ethnic guidelines. 'At least there was no hypocrisy about it,' Kirk wrote in an article for the *Los Angeles Times* in 1977,* '. . . I couldn't get a job delivering newspapers because I was a Jew, and no Jew was allowed to work at the

**Where 'Gentlemen's Agreements' Still Reign*, by Kirk Douglas.

largest factory in town. No one bothered to hide behind a mask of false piety, however. They were painfully direct.'

Herschel, too uneducated and too Jewish to secure a steady job making carpets, supplemented his occasional mill work by peddling fruit, vegetables, fuel, and junk. He spent long days toiling through the streets of Amsterdam with his horse and wagon, hawking his wares and scavenging for scrap metal. 'I had friends in New York later who used to tell me their fathers kept horses,' Kirk told Katie Kelly in *Interview* magazine in 1974. 'They meant race horses, for God's sake. And I'd tell them my father had a horse too . . . and a cart and a load of vegetables!'

The other six Danielovitch kids had something in common which Kirk would never share – they were exclusively female. His three older sisters – Ruth, Fritzi, and Ida – were followed by three younger ones: Marion, Betty, and Catherine. Kirk found himself in the difficult 'middle child' position, surrounded by a sea of women. He was like a genetic hiccup on the Danielovitch family tree, and he didn't enjoy it at all. 'We laugh at it now, but it was terrible being the only male in a house full of women,' he explains. 'I was dying to get out. In a sense, it lit a fire under me. It's said that an actor is the kind of actor he is because of his childhood and his life experiences, and that it's possible to gauge his strength and his weaknesses in view of that background. I think this is certainly true in my own case.'

Kirk's desire to escape probably made the working world appear more tempting. Although his school/work days were long, they provided ample independence and a welcome opportunity to exert a small degree of control over his life. Kirk peddled soda and snacks to mill owners, sold newspapers, or played the delivery boy, the messenger, whatever he could find. When he wasn't actually plying his given trade-of-the-day, he fantasised. 'I became something of a dreamer . . . I didn't have time to play, I had to have my fun in imagining.'

However, unpleasant developments in the world outside the Danielovitch household also contributed to the youngster's flights from reality. 'I was about eleven years old when a bunch of kids pounced on me one day, beating me bloody and yelling: "You killed Jesus Christ." When my mother asked me what happened, I wailed: "They said I killed Jesus Christ and I don't even know who he is." '

In his limited leisure time, Kirk and his pal Pete Riccie wandered around town, confiding their respective yearnings and escape plans. Pete wanted to be a big wheel, a politician, and Kirk wanted to be anything . . . as long as it carried him far away from Amsterdam. 'I tried to escape the poverty of my life by escaping into daydreams. I guess I got into the habit permanently – what better way to live in a daydream than by being an actor.'

At home, disparate parental opinions towards Kirk's future and present responsibilities added to his woes. Bryna insisted on education first and foremost, even though time spent in school meant less money in the family coffer. Herschel adhered to the old-country philosophy: he insisted his boy work full-time. Kirk wasn't the powerhouse his papa was (Herschel was the best fighter in the neighbourhood, if not the town) and could never be satisfied with a trade depending solely on manual labour.

Whatever Herschel's expectations for his only son entailed, Kirk never seemed to live up to them, at least not as far as Kirk could ascertain. Papa Danielovitch didn't lavish praise upon any of his offspring. In the end, Bryna provided all the comfort and nurturing; father and son grew apart.

Grade school recitations and small parts in plays provided Kirk's first taste of the footlights. But the driving desire to act didn't take hold until he entered Wilbur Lynch High School and came under the influence of Louise Livingstone, an English teacher. A field trip to Albany (the nearest cosmopolitan venue) to see Katherine Cornell star in *The Barretts of Wimpole Street* exposed Kirk to the full impact of a professional troupe's performance.

Bryna's motherly enthusiasm and Ms Livingstone's teacherly encouragement and advice gave Kirk a focal point for his energetic temperament and ambitious nature. Ms Livingstone pointed him towards practical exercises to bolster his academic record and prepare him for a career in 'show biz.' Kirk joined the debating team, refined his tone in speech competitions, studied plays, and other aspects of actors and the theatre.*

Meanwhile, relations between Herschel and Kirk steadily deteriorated. The elder Danielovitch didn't seem to appreciate his son's achievements and growing sense of self-worth and confidence; it was perhaps inevitable that the undercurrent of tension between the two would bob to the surface.

One night, Kirk, in what was to become a characteristic to-hell-with-it-all outburst of pent-up irritation, catapulted a spoonful of wet tea leaves into his father's face. Herschel snapped out of his customary sullen silence and flung his son across the room, expressively demonstrating the possible results of gaining his complete attention. Kirk rose relatively unharmed physically – and much improved mentally – by his gesture of defiance toward the mysterious stranger who was his father.

Kirk's dramatic recitation of a poem reflecting the thoughts of a dying soldier won him first place (and his first real laurel for acting) in a Sanford Mills-sponsored competition. His boss at the Goldmeer Wholesale Company was so impressed, he

*Over the years, Kirk kept in touch with Ms Livingstone and credited her (along with his mother) in almost every interview for his early inspiration. As a further gesture of gratitude, he wrote a foreword to a book of her poetry.

requested an encore presentation for some of the company's employees.

Bryna continued to stand behind Kirk and his determination to act, but she never lost sight of other priorities. Kirk recalls, 'When I signed my first big contract with a studio, I called my mother up to tell her. "Come home," she said. "You look so thin in the movies. You aren't getting enough to eat." But it wasn't only food for the body she cared about. Food for the mind also counted with her. She had never gone to school and my getting an education was terribly important to her. I taught her to write her name.'

To Bryna, getting an education meant attending college, so she insisted that Kirk keep his grades up. A bright student, he juggled homework, money-work, and his dramatic activities quite well. After graduating from high school he expected to find a way to attend university, but a major complication developed – Herschel ran away from home.

Saddled with the unforeseen burden of being 'man of the house,' Kirk temporarily shelved his collegiate plans and went to work full-time in Lurie's Department Store. Sometimes he sold goods in the men's section, which wasn't unbearable, but the tedious chore of window-washing drove him to distraction on a daily basis. 'There always seemed to be one more to wash,' he remembers. 'I think that was the most depressing year of my life.' A co-worker clued him into the shortcut of washing every other window, instead of doing them all at once, but the entire experience was debilitating, and frustrating. Kirk contributed the lion's share of his earnings towards the maintenance of the family, but he managed to stash away a few kopecks for school. A year's labour yielded less than $170 – a sum as insufficient for tuition then as it would be today.

From a logical standpoint, the situation seemed completely impossible, so Kirk planned a totally harebrained coup to get what he wanted . . . and another facet of the Douglas/Danielovitch myth was carved.

With his shoes shined and his jaw set, Kirk put out his thumb and hitched to St Lawrence University in Canton, New York. Unfortunately, his last ride came from a guy hauling a load of fertiliser, and by the time Kirk gained entry to the dean's office, he felt and smelled the worse for where he'd been.

Nonetheless, the dean found Kirk's school records impressive, and he agreed to enrol him without an application, promising to arrange a loan and a work/study schedule. Kirk was elated; he'd taken a chance, and reaped greater rewards than he'd ever hoped for. Henceforth, going for the long shot was a primary part of his modus operandi.

After a brief turn as a gardener, courtesy of the National Youth Administration, Kirk moved on to equally exciting part-time employment. His next job offered a fringe benefit; as a janitor he avoided the expense of a room in the college dorms (which he couldn't afford in any case) by napping in the custodian's quarters.

In his four years at St Lawrence, Kirk reigned as president of the student body,* president of the German Club, an intercollegiate wrestling champ, and president of the drama society. 'That did it,' he said in 1974. 'I don't want to be president of anything.'

Because of these laurels, one of the frat houses loosened their exclusionary noose and extended an offer of so-called 'house privileges' to President Douglas. 'I could pay dues, eat meals, live at the house, even attend fraternity dances. But I could

*No ordinary feat, for Jews were excluded from certain campus activities at the same time, like fraternities. Kirk seems somewhat surprised by his election still. He calls it 'a strange fluke – a change in the system of voting . . .' and gleefully admits 'the Alumni Association was *furious*.'

not attend their meetings, and I guess they wouldn't have taught me the secret handshake. I declined the kind invitation.'

During the summer he did what he could for a buck, even working as a carnival wrestler. (Posed as a member of the audience, Kirk waited until the 'bad guy' was winning by foul and dastardly means, then leapt into the ring, challenged the bastard, and performed feats of derring-do.)

When he wasn't acting in the ring, he pursued whatever interesting roles the university drama society could offer and rear-viewed details of stagecraft as stage manager. These days he sported the moniker Isadore Demsky.

When he graduated from St Lawrence in 1939, Issur Danielovitch/Isadore Demsky possessed a BA, a desire to attend the prestigious American Academy of Dramatic Arts in New York City, and, maybe on a good day, two pennies to rub together.

A repeat performance was in order; Kirk hitched up his shorts and attacked the Academy with the same guerilla tactics he'd used on the university. After extensive begging, wheedling, hard-sell, and an impressive audition, he managed to win acceptance *and* convince the board to create a new scholarship for his benefit and edification. It was here that Kirk Douglas officially left Issur Danielovitch and Isadore Demsky behind.*

Kirk's macho-vellian trials made Ms Bacall (who was, after all, a nice young Jewish girl with a comparatively idyllic upbringing) an even bigger Kirk Douglas fan. She wanted to do whatever she could for this charming, handsome, and broke individual – and he gladly submitted to her heartfelt generosity.

In his first year at the AADA, Kirk resided at the Greenwich

*It's been indicated that the name 'Kirk Douglas' was suggested by Mrs Karl Malden, who, along with her husband, did time with Isadore Demsky in a summer-stock production. Other sources assert that Mr Douglas concocted it himself. In any case, everyone admits that the surname is borrowed from Douglas Fairbanks, Sr.

Settlement House, tutoring drama in exchange for room and board. By the time he met Lauren, his increased workload from the Academy precluded this comfortable situation, and Kirk occupied a closet-size room on Third Street which cost him $2.50 a month.

Lauren dated Kirk whenever she was asked. She brought him to her grandmother's house for dinner sometimes (he and Grandma got on as well as he and Mom Bacall did) and he met her uncle Charlie, who kindly passed on a cast-off winter coat to Kirk.

In her autobiography, Ms Bacall fondly remembers visions of domestic bliss-to-be as she sat on Kirk's floor, mending a straying button onto his gift-coat. By her own assessment, she was a little girl who blew everything out of proportion in her dreams. After she fell for Bogart, she realized that 'every emotional involvement I'd had before – like Kirk . . . I'd thought was love, but it wasn't. . . .'

In the meantime, it would have to suffice. Ms Bacall continued to daydream of their future together, acting together, being together . . . and Kirk continued to be friendly, but somewhat distant. An age discrepancy of about ten years was a consideration, and Ms Bacall wasn't experienced in the ways of men and their hormones. Her idea of going quite far enough consisted of a few simple manoeuvres: 'Necking in dark corners was about my speed. . . .'

One night, things almost got out of hand when Kirk attempted to have his way with the cow-eyed teenager. 'He was hell on ladies back then,' Ms Bacall explained in *US* magazine. 'I turned him down because nice Jewish girls don't make love until they're married. And by the way, I would call it a little bit more than a pass. He was being rather forceful, feeling his oats. Kirk was a very lively fellow. That's fine, but not for a frightened fifteen-year-old girl.' It was obvious to both Ms

Bacall and Mr Douglas that her desire wouldn't be overcome by her hesitance and immaturity.

Lauren became pals with a senior at the Academy, a lovely woman named Diana Dill. One night when she stayed at Diana's apartment, 'Kirk's name came into the conversation. She said, "Oh, don't ever get mixed up with anyone like him. You'll get hurt. Actors are unreliable. Not really to be trusted. He's all right to have fun with – don't get serious about him." '

Fortunately, Lauren didn't blab her inner yearnings for the dashing Mr Douglas to Ms Dill; later, Lauren discovered that Kirk and Diana were dating rather seriously. Ms Bacall's entrance had occurred during some sort of romantic rift.

When Kirk entered the Navy and found himself far from home, he wrote to Lauren occasionally, '. . . letters I wanted to receive. They were written out of loneliness, I knew, but I adored having them.' As it turned out, Lauren Bacall did play an important part in Kirk's life, but not as his leading lady fair, onstage or off.

Lauren Bacall wasn't the only beautiful woman frequenting the Eighty-sixth Street Schrafft's where Kirk waitered and bussed tables; another 'often seen' at the counter was Diana Dill. Diana was born on January 22, 1923, in Bermuda, the daughter of its Crown Solicitor, Thomas Neville Dill and Ruth Rapalje Dill (née Neilson). Kirk met her at the Academy and spent their on-off dating relationship alternately sparring and pitching woo; but no permanent arrangement came from their initial liaison.

Kirk Douglas graduated from the AADA in 1941 with one thing on his mind: Broadway. With his usual aplomb, he targeted several possibilities and zeroed in on producer Guthrie McClintic, who wanted to know if he could sing. Kirk's first reward for two hard years of intensive dramatic training amounted to a walk-on as a singing messengerboy in *Spring Again*. Whatever indignities he suffered yodeling 'Yankee Doodle' were probably sufficiently counterbalanced by the thrill of finally appearing on Broadway. In any case, it certainly beat the hell out of his second 'part'. As stage manager for Katherine Cornell's production of Chekhov's *The Three Sisters*, he provided nothing more substantial than an off-stage echo.

This slow start didn't discourage Kirk's plans to steadily plough his way towards a successful and fulfilling career on the stage until he received notice of his third part – in a telegram which began 'Greetings . . .' He packed his belongings and elected the life of a seafaring man in the Navy. This meant yet another year of education – training at the Notre Dame University midshipman school.

After graduation, Kirk Douglas, Naval-Ensign-At-Large, found himself provided with free transportation to the beautiful Pacific Ocean, where he and his fellow crewmates spent late '42 and most of '43 hunting submarines. Eventually, they found one. Kirk's unit was chasing a Japanese sub through shallow waters, tossing depth charges overboard. One of the charges blew prematurely. 'We almost blew our own ship out of the water! It was my fault. I phoned a man to hurl a depth charge marker into the sea, but my voice was no good and the man "obeyed" by throwing a live depth charge instead, which fell practically at my feet. I got thrown against a stack, and woke up in a hospital where penicillin was about my only meal for the next five months.' He sustained a litany of serious internal damages, abrasions, and haemorrhages; the Navy shipped what was left of him to recuperate in Balboa Hospital at the San Diego naval station. As an additional insult to his battered body, Kirk suffered a severe bout of dysentery. Though he said nothing at the time, some of his later films made his feelings about war in general quite clear.

The only pleasant interlude in the grim months of ex-Naval Ensign Kirk Douglas's recovery came courtesy of Ms Diana Dill. According to 'the myth', Kirk saw Diana's picture on the cover of *Life* magazine, tracked her down, persuaded her to visit him, and wound up proposing. The exact details are perhaps a shade less dramatic, but whatever the circumstances of their prenuptials, Kirk and Diana married on November 2, 1943.

If nothing else, this semi-mismatch completely supported Bryna's vision of America as a classless society. The former Miss Dill originated from a 'posh' family, and acquired her education from several prestigious English academies, receiving her certificate from the Cambridge School. Although it's difficult to imagine in these 'enlightened' times, Kirk's marriage to Diana must have seemed comparable to your next-door neighbour marrying royalty.

In 1944, after Kirk's official discharge from the Service, the Douglases crossed country back to New York City, and hopefully the stage, for they both intended to establish careers on Broadway. On June 29, 1944, Kirk made his first tentative step when he replaced Richard Widmark in *Kiss and Tell* at the Biltmore Theater. He adopted the role of Lieutenant Lenny Archer, 'the eloping young aviator'. Diana embarked on a career of a different sort than the one she'd originally anticipated: motherhood-to-be.

Following *Kiss and Tell*, Douglas appeared in *Trio* and *Star in the Window*, neither of which benefitted from critical acclaim or extended runs. His next foray, *Alice in Arms*, pleased critics but not audiences: Kirk found comfort in the good notices he collected for his portrayal of an Army sergeant. However, the role Kirk passed on during this period is the one which made Broadway history.

George Abbott, the director of *Kiss and Tell*, approached Kirk one day and asked him if he could 'sing loud'. When Douglas replied yes, Abbott pointed him toward an audition for *On the Town.* Blissfully ignorant and absolutely unhindered by his complete inexperience as a singer, he shouted out one of the score's now-familiar tunes and got the part. When he actually realised the multiple complexities of Leonard Bernstein's music, the choreography, and the whole damn thing, he suddenly developed laryngitis; it lasted until they recast the part. Kirk still held hope for a chance at a musical, but as he put it, 'How many musicals can you do when you can't sing and dance?'

Glad tidings from the homefront came when Diana gave birth to Michael Kirk Douglas on September 25, 1944. With another mouth to feed, Kirk supplemented his stage work with forays into radio, where he honed his vocal skills and picked up a decent wage.

While Kirk involved himself with his new kid and his new role as the Unknown Soldier in *The Wind Is Ninety*, wheels churned in Hollywood. Producer Hal B. Wallis of Paramount Studios desired fresh talent, and one Ms Lauren Bacall advised him to eyeball her ex-flame on his upcoming trip to New York. And so it came to be that Kirk Douglas, who probably bore more war wounds than acting credits, was offered a motion picture contract . . . and turned it down. Spoon-fed theatre at the AADA, trained in Shakespeare and the mighty Greeks, Kirk couldn't perceive of himself as a movie star. So he continued with *The Wind Is Ninety*, temporarily ignoring Hollywood's call.

After the play closed, Douglas's expectations of further work remained just that. When nothing materialised, he began to wonder about that contract-dangling producer's intentions, so he placed a call. Wallis wanted a screen test; Douglas flew out to provide one.

The Strange Loves of Martha Ivers gave Kirk his first on screen experience and his first leading role all in one neat package.

Unlike his later image, he played the weed to Barbara Stanwyck's poison-ivy murderess. This well-received, film-noir-ish soaper provided Kirk with an auspicious debut indeed, and Paramount with a potential star for their stable. . . . Or so they believed.

Instead of following up his initial success with another picture, Kirk returned to New York to take part in Bella and Sam Spewack's satirical piece of poop, *Woman Bites Dog*, which lasted all of two nights. Years later, he still felt the sting of rejection. 'In a sense, I'm a failure,' he told *Newsday's* Mike McGrady in 1963. 'When I was young that was my whole dream, to be a stage actor. I went from Hollywood to Broadway just once . . . and flopped. Still a movie, you do it and it's months before you know. On the stage the rewards, if there are rewards, are immediate.'

On January 23, 1947, Diana bore another son, Joel. Realities enforced by this latest addition probably influenced the proud father's decision to return to Hollywood, where a contract with Hal Wallis assured him of a steady $500 a week. When Paramount couldn't find a suitable vehicle for him, they hired him out to RKO. There he played second fiddle to Robert Mitchum in the classic *Out of the Past* and established himself as the perfect 'suave bastard'-type. This immaculate film was followed by an overblown, expensive dud, *Mourning Becomes Electra*, which did zilch for Kirk career-wise; but he redeemed himself with *I Walk Alone*, co-starring with another Wallis inmate, Burt Lancaster.

Redemption came not from the film itself, but from the interplay between Burt and Kirk. They disliked the movie, hated their roles, and argued with everyone; but they got along like gangbusters. An unholy alliance was formed, and its effect on the movie *almost* saved it.

Meanwhile, Diana made moves towards establishing herself

in the professional scheme of things, but a role in *The Hasty Heart* (staged in Santa Barbara) and a small part in *Sign of the Ram* were her sole efforts in 1948. A schism appeared in the fabric of the Douglas union; Diana wanted to work, Kirk wanted her to stay at home with the kids.

Chapter Two

FROM SHORTS TO THE SCREEN

'Life must be a challenge or where's the meaning. Hell, if I wanted to play it safe, I wouldn't have been an actor.'

– Kirk Douglas, '63

'I spent my summers with my father or went on location with him. And I could see how he handled himself. His business is, and was, being a "movie star" as well as a producer. . . . I saw him at parties with other stars. I saw them as real people, trying to conduct their lives in some sort of health despite the tension. . . . Those things were the real strength of being brought up in the business.'

– Michael Douglas '78

'I made a career, in a sense, of being an SOB,' Kirk Douglas told the *American Weekly* in 1962. 'Look at *Champion*. The guy punched his crippled brother and raped his ex-wife. But at the preview the people cheered him in his big fight scene. People know my guy is no good but understand how he got that way. He's usually a rebel against society, and most of us would like to say, "To hell with society".'

Kirk Douglas identifies strongly with *Champion*, the movie

which made him a star and won him his first Oscar nomination. *Champion* proved Kirk's theory that one can buck the system and reap great rewards, even in Hollywood with its power structures, chain of command, and strict protocol.

When Stanley Kramer showed Kirk the script for *Champion*, the producer made it quite clear that Douglas wouldn't receive the kind of money he'd become accustomed to if he took the role. Meanwhile, MGM stood in the background, offering a supporting part in *The Great Sinner* (with Ava Gardner and Gregory Peck) and $50,000. With everyone chorusing. 'You're nuts!' Kirk grabbed the lead in *Champion* and walked away a winner.

While Kirk Douglas's career soared, his marriage went down the tubes. Diana still wanted to act, and began to feel somewhat ill at ease with her circumstances. Although Kirk genuinely cared about her and his sons, making every effort to be a good father and applauding Michael and Joel's smallest accomplishments, he wasn't eager for his wife to share the spotlight as anything other than his wife.

While some title-tattle credited the marital breakdown to the effect of success on Kirk's ego, Diana explained, 'It's too hard on a man who wants to be the breadwinner to find himself with a career woman. My wanting to act was an assertion of my own independence – maybe in defiance of Kirk's success, maybe in defence of it.' Kirk insisted, 'Our marriage was coming apart at the seams long before *Champion*.'

'Doug was a perfectionist . . . and I was a happy-go-lucky,' Diana recalls. 'I'd potter around the house in bare feet. His resentment over that childlike action was justified when I dropped a dish on my feet and was bedridden three weeks. . . . On such things our temperaments clashed . . . so we separated and I was on my own again. I had grown dependent upon Doug in six years of marriage. I wanted to fill the void of the "nothingness" that happens after a marriage ends. Drifting frightened me and out of my fear grew maturity.' Ms Dill began the long hike toward success on her own, and over the years she managed to build a steady career on stage, in movies, and television. Michael and Joel spent some of their childhood watching their mother rehearse in theatres while they kept each other company.

Their divorce didn't fall into the typical instantaneous clichéd 'Hollywood' category. At first, they attempted a reconciliation, playing down the press reports of a permanent separation. Diana, Michael, and Joel stayed in their house in Laurel Canyon and Kirk moved to a small rental nearby, so he could continue to see the boys and his wife almost every day. In interviews, he didn't deny the split, but lamented the loss of his privacy at such a sensitive time. 'My wife and I are not scowling at each other. We're *not* getting a divorce,' Kirk stated firmly. 'Diana and I have a problem similar to the problem many married couples in Podunk or Ashtabula face and work out. Simply this and nothing more. . . . *I am constantly hoping* that we may work out our problems too.'

Unfortunately for those involved, the Douglas break-up couldn't be glued back together. Diana officially divorced Kirk in Los Angeles on February 8, 1950, and she and the boys were soon on their way to a new life in New York.

The divorce, with its unpleasant reminders of his parents' failed marriage, sent Kirk into analysis in an honestly valiant effort to resolve his feelings. His second wife Anne once remarked, 'Part of my husband's life has been a monstrous effort to prove himself and gain recognition in the eyes of his father. . . . Not even four years of psychoanalysis . . . could alter the drives that began as a desire to prove himself.' She also cited his childhood in a somewhat matriarchal, predominantly female household. 'There are other complications. He needed to get away from female domination. That is why . . . I have to be careful and not let him think I am taking over.'

Mr Douglas expressed his views on working women in his own abrupt way to Ed Preston of *Parade* magazine in June of 1952: 'What upsets me about modern women is . . . they're still fighting a so-called battle for emancipation . . . and I don't think they really want to win that battle.' He explained that while he understood certain women's need to work for financial reasons, or because some absolutely awesome talent drove them, he couldn't condone career women in any case because 'a career woman is competing with men. And when she does this, it's a very unusual woman who doesn't compromise her femininity in some way.

'Just being a woman and a wife is a career,' Douglas continued. 'Instead of trying to develop talents to compete with men, women should train themselves to complement men. I'm appalled by how little women know about how to run a home . . . I may be too proud of men but I'm convinced they're superior to women. . . . To my way of thinking, the greatest thing about women should be simply – *they're women.*' Kirk went on to utter the immortal words, 'Don't get me wrong. I love women. I think women are here to stay.' As for the 'fair sex' in general, Kirk reflected on the increase in his fan mail when he played the heel on screen: 'I believe women are attracted to cruelty. They don't want gentleness and tenderness.'

Michael and Joel, former candidates for the dubious accolades of growing up in Beverly Hills, began their new life on Central Park West, not far from Kirk and Diana's alma mater. Michael attended the Alan Stevenson School on Seventy-eighth Street and Lexington Avenue, where the strict dress code relegated him to a uniform of white shirt, tie, a blazer, and grey flannel shorts or pants.

Diana felt enthusiastic about their new surroundings and the promise of a fresh start. 'I went to New York to do a television drama and decided I wanted to live in the East where I could start again. Luckily, I found an apartment near Central Park. I furnished it myself and converted the dining room into a playroom for the boys. . . . On Sundays we went horseback riding in the park.'

Kirk stayed very much in the picture, writing and calling from wherever he was, and of course they visited during vacations. The shifting from coast to coast affected both boys. 'We had to develop an emotional toughness travelling between our two different worlds,' Michael recalled in 1985. Fortunately, this instability didn't produce unhealthy results; instead, it bonded the brothers and created a solid partnership.

Genuine trauma resulted indirectly from Diana's decision to accept a proffered acting contract in California. Michael exited from his sheltered world for life among the peasants in a public junior high school, where he skipped from fifth to seventh grade. His clothes were wrong, everyone was older than he, there were gangs, and the first girl he kissed surprised the hell out of him by keeping her mouth open. Michael ended up in the Black Fox Military Academy in Los Angeles.

Michael tends to downplay the aftermath of his parents' divorce. 'People always talk about the effect a divorce has on the kids,' Michael said once. 'Often the parents suffer more. Kids can handle anything as long as they're loved, and I was always loved.' On the other hand, Kirk has admitted, 'When Diana and I divorced, he was old enough to be affected. Only in the last few years have we become friends, and I feel a warmth.' Sadly, Kirk seems to have interpreted Michael's feelings as dislike, but Michael responds: 'No, there was no great dislike, I just didn't let anyone rattle my cage. I was trying to live my own life. I didn't give out too easily. . . .' Later, Michael would become even more vague and evasive about the matter, perhaps as an attempt to privatise an already too-public matter.

Kirk and Diana tried to maintain a smooth ship and not push and pull at their children too much. Kirk especially tried to refrain from using the luxury of their upbringing against them. 'I'd bite my tongue before I'd start preaching to them about how rough I had it as a kid,' he attested in the *National Enquirer* in 1974. 'I've seen more fathers lose their children's attention and respect by saying that than in any other way. I stood in line in the Bowery to get a Thanksgiving dinner for twenty cents, and at a rescue mission to get a free Christmas dinner . . . but my poverty was an advantage in many respects. I was desperate to get out of it . . . it gave me drive and ambition.'

Whether he waved his hardships under his sons' noses or not, Kirk's past is a matter of public record and therefore accessible to one and all, including his children. After divorce proceedings finalised and buried the marital union of Kirk and Diana, other aspects of the virile Mr Douglas's life became equally regarded as a matter of public record and interest – namely, his 'love life'.

In 1953, when columnist Sidney Skolsky asked Kirk what kind of girl he was looking for (after his divorce from Diana), the film star replied, 'I have been looking for her so long that I have forgotten what it is I'm supposed to find.' This served Kirk as a stock, evasive answer for his four years of bachelorhood, while he worked his way through several very public and sometimes totally tabloid-manufactured romances. Rightly or wrongly, Kirk found himself saddled with the yoke of the Hollywood Lothario, and he couldn't dance with a woman in public without rumours springing up. It annoyed him, and it was probably extremely vexing for Michael and Joel.

Under the heading 'Romances That Failed,' one movie mag detailed (in a melodramatic, romantic, and almost surreal fashion) the rise and fall of the Douglas/Pier Angeli debacle thus: 'A man's entitled to his hobbies. Kirk collects living dolls. He collected Gardner (pre-Sinatra), Tierney (pre-Aly Khan), Hayworth (pre-Haymes). These ladies entered the game on his own terms. Pier Angeli didn't. She gave him her trusting heart.

'Of course she should have known better. Mama warned her. But the miracle of first love dawns to a man's tenderness, quickens to his touch, and has little to do with mothers. He was thirty-six when it started, she was twenty. Not a date-wise American twenty. An Italian twenty, peeking shyly out from under the maternal wing. She's a quieter Pier today, whose eyes hold a new hurt. Sure she'll get over it. Girls have died and worms have eaten them though not for love. Pier in her innocence saw love conquering all. Kirk in his worldliness knew it never could. Her first love cried for cherishing hands. I wish he'd picked on someone his own size.'

In the midst of such folderol and its implications of Hollywood Hun-dom, Kirk tried to maintain an air of civilised and gentlemanly dignity. Post-Pier, his public comments on her were limited to compliments like 'She's one of the most beautiful girls I've ever met.' He allowed general utterances about his likes and dislikes, such as 'European women feel that the man is more important . . . they cater to him, and make him feel comfortable. They don't argue about equality.' Occasionally, a personal note would slip through. 'American men are the most romantic in the world,' he explained soon after he and Ms Angeli parted, '. . . when we fall – we fall hard.'

Diana remembers some of the confusion which resulted from Kirk's liaisons. 'Whenever Kirk's name was coupled with a girl's in a gossip column, people rushed to tell me to get my reaction. I said nothing, but kept busy with the children, the house, and acting.' One day Michael gave his summation of stepmothers. 'They're wicked,' he said, 'like in *Cinderella.*' 'No, Michael,' Diana replied. 'They can be kind and if Daddy marries again, you'll have a good stepmother.'

One Christmas Kirk visited his family with a woman who friends considered a likely candidate for wife number two, a rich Californian divorcee named Irene Wrightman McEvoy. Things didn't pan out for the couple, but the visit helped Diana come to some conclusions. 'Seeing us all together I knew I had found myself . . . I could face facts and assume responsibility at last. I had built a new life, was running it and making my own decisions. My children were happy, my husband and I were friends and I wanted him to have happiness, too. I know now that one has to earn it.'

For all his care, things reached a peak when Kirk's name became linked with a Mrs Estelle Auguste, a forty-two-year-old filthy-rich Florida widow who implied that an invitation of some sort extended to Mr Douglas contributed to the cancellation of her engagement to former heavyweight boxer Jack Dempsey. The media had a great time with the alleged monkey-biz, as accusations, denials, and the clipped responses of Kirk's rising irritation flew thick and fast. A mention of Mrs Auguste even wormed its way into Kirk's second marriage announcement.

Kirk Douglas met Anne Buydens, a remarkable woman to say the least, on the set of the French production, *Act of Love.* Anne, serving as publicity representative for her friend, director Anatole Litvak, almost immediately encountered the active Mr Douglas. Impressed by his 'ferocious vitality', but wary of his reputation and occupation, the wily Mrs Buydens (a recent divorcee) began a fencing match which resulted in one of Hollywood's most successful unions.

Like Kirk, Anne is a survivor. She beat death in the Second World War by convincing Nazi soldiers that she was a German girl, she made it through one unfortunate marriage, she learned to live with Kirk's explosive artistic temperament, and she even became a business asset to him, wielding and balancing the power of his complex professional and personal monetary affairs. But one of her most difficult and admirable moves concerned her cooperation in incorporating the East and West Coast Douglas families.

When Anne and Kirk tied the knot on May 29, 1954 in Las Vegas, it signalled the end of Kirk's wild oats spree (which Anne had endured partially, since it overlapped with her entrance into the scene) and his 'occupation' as press target.

This turn of events must have simultaneously relieved and worried Michael and Joel. True, the public attention focused on their single father was a breeding ground for all kinds of potentially uncomfortable incidents, but what child doesn't harbour apprehension of the classically villainesque, interloping step-parent?

Although the new Mrs Douglas seems to have easily slid around many of the typical problems of stepmotherhood, the survival of the Douglases as a solid but expandable unit is the result of a cooperative effort on the parts of the adults involved. The oft-bandied and seldom actually productive idea of regulating behaviour 'for the children's sake' combined with everyone's desire to maintain their public dignity and private peace added up to an extended family who simultaneously cared and supported while allowing the separate entities breathing space.

While some found the friendship between Anne and Diana and their reluctance to indulge in verbal hair-pulling unusual, all parties involved retained a poker-faced nonchalance. 'Why shouldn't we be on good terms?' Anne would innocently reply to probing reporters. 'Both our divorces were congenial affairs. And we all like each other.' She seems to have realised that any interference on her part or attempts to come between Kirk and his ex-wife and sons would have proved futile and disastrous. 'He has a sense of loyalty and responsibility to his family which borders on a guilt complex. You don't have to be a psychiatrist to realise this is a compensation for his own father's lack of loyalty and responsibility. . . . Kirk is first and foremost a family man.' As an adult with a child of his own, Michael explained, 'When my mother and father got divorced, they each remarried . . . and the four of them are best friends. . . . I guess it depends on what you're used to. I'm not saying that it's easy, but if you've treasured the time you've spent with someone, you'll want to stay in touch.'

On November 23, 1955, Peter Vincent Douglas was born to Anne and Kirk. Eric Anthony, the final component of the second generation of the Douglas Dynasty, followed on June 21, 1958. In spite of the age differences and the possible jealousies inherent in such situations, Michael and Joel and Peter and Eric developed healthy systems for dealing with one another and nurturing their own particular versions of brotherly love.

On December 14, 1956, William Darrid, a theatrical producer and writer, officially became Michael and Joel's stepfather. Unlike Kirk, William didn't find Diana's theatrical aspirations problematic, and, in addition, he managed to forge a fine relationship with his two stepsons. Michael cites him as 'a powerful influence on our life'. Bill Darrid and his new family retreated to the steady suburban world of Westport, Connecticut, which must have seemed heavenly after Michael's disturbing sabbatical in California. Although Joel and Michael still commuted between their parents' disparate lifestyles, their stepfather provided a necessary counterbalance and generally stabilising force.

Michael resumed his private education in old established pre-preps like the Deerfield Academy (an all-boy facility based in Massachusetts) and Choate, a co-ed Ivy-League prep school located in Wallingford, Connecticut.

Kirk maintains that Michael is, in certain ways, the least ambitious of his children. Michael tended to drift off into the stratosphere. 'I was captain of the ninth-grade football team and it was all down-hill from there,' he says half-jokingly. 'I went from first string to third string. They used to say, "Douglas may be light, but he's slow." '

Michael also enjoyed participating in his school band, wielding a trumpet until a profusion of similarly inclined students pushed him towards the trombone. To this day he retains a healthy interest in both sports and a wide spectrum of musical categories, including classical.

After graduation, his plans swung in a wide arc – literally from coast to coast. 'I was to go to Yale, but I didn't like too much where I was at then . . .' he told reporter Jerry Tallmer in 1971. Later he recalled, 'I was not very happy, I was an introverted, uptight kind of kid.' He remembers his adviser at Choate fanning around several brochures, and one from the University of California at Santa Barbara caught his wandering attention. It featured a photo of a surfboard-toting dude strolling down the beach with not one, but two bikini-clad dudettes. In 1963, bikinis were a practically unknown species on the East Coast, and the potential of observing them on living, womanly beings interested Michael deeply. 'I heard that this school had a ratio of three girls to every one boy. So I went there . . .'

Predictably, this attitude didn't bode well for the old grade point average. 'I was all over the place,' he admits. Diving into the relative freedom of college after the restrictive life of private school gave Michael a case of the academic bends. 'On a four point system, I got a 1.4 the first semester, 1.9 the second . . .' Understandably, the school considered a year's absence beneficial to both parties, and Michael departed rather unceremoniously. 'Later on, what made me realise I had made it was when they made me Alumnus of the Year. Oh yeah, they let me back in after a while – you know that thing, where they let you have time off to mature.'

Michael decided to mature back home in Westport, Connecticut, in a Mobil gas station. 'I always liked cars,' he told *Parade* magazine in 1988. This love for automobiles led him into a hot-rod club, the Downshifters. According to an article in *Cosmopolitan*, the Downshifters' nifty diversification consisted of a thing called Midnight Auto, which specialised in hot parts . . . not of the dramatic variety. His major achievement during this period was making 'Mobile Man of the Month' – and he's still got the plaque to prove it.

The eldest sprig of the Douglas family tree was rapidly sprouting into a potential bad seed. Like many of his peer group, Michael drifted through the mid-sixties in an aimless fashion; lost and waiting for something, *anything*, to happen.

A little fatherly intervention plucked Michael from the being and nothingness of Westport and plopped him into the midst of more rigorous climes. Kirk brought Michael to England and Norway to work with the crew of his latest, *The Heroes of Telemark*. The English portion of the project forced no hardship on anyone, but conditions in Norway were somewhat less appealing; there were plenty of snowballs and skiing, combined with subzero temperatures, to be had by all.

Immediately afterwards, the Douglases ventured to Israel, the setting of *Cast a Giant Shadow*. Michael's title read 'Assistant Director,' but basically he functioned as a gofer. In spite of the limited range of responsibilities, Michael began to acquire an interest in the business.

After his year abroad, sort of a theatrical version of a southern gentleman's Grand Tour, Michael returned to Santa Barbara and elected to move into a commune in an area known as

Mountain Drive, a situation which pleased his father no end. 'He screamed at me,' Michael remembers. At this point, Kirk continued to harbour hope that Michael would settle back into his prep-school persona and rekindle his adolescent inclinations towards a respectable career as a lawyer (one gets the impression that this idea came much more from the mind of the senior Mr Douglas; Michael never really directly refers to any such desire on his own part). Although it's completely anachronistic and difficult to imagine, Michael's soirée in the wilderness was considered completely scandalous at the time, especially because of his background.

The concerned father made one visit to Mountain Drive. Michael roomed above the kitchen, in a separate building from the main house. The guest of honour got the bed, while the host bunked on the floor. When Kirk wanted to take a leak, he was informed that one had a choice of hiking to the main house or simply making use of the balcony, which overlooked a particularly wild and bushy expanse of Californian tropical growth. While electing to make use of the former facility, Douglas began to laugh and when Michael enquired, he replied, 'Listen son, this is what I've been trying to get away from my whole life.'

During this stretch of time, the relationship between father and son began to crystallise, and aspects of past hurts and disappointments rose to the surface. Kirk had, in his own confusion concerning his past as absentee father, handed both Joel and Michael mixed messages. While he encouraged them to work by giving them small jobs on his movies, he actively campaigned to discourage either from adopting an attraction for life under the lights. In many ways, Dad represented the perfect role model; the self-made man who dragged himself from the dirt to the limelight. But the phoenix-like rise of his father initially cowed Michael, and the overall effect was a negative one. After he'd made some significant inroads into the business himself, Michael told Alan Ebert in 1979, 'My old man wasn't just Kirk Douglas but this enormous being, this dynamic, magnetic presence. Damned if he wasn't Spartacus himself. I never felt I could measure up to my dad or be anything like him, so I quit trying. I dropped out, stopped competing and became the opposite of everything he was.'

This desire to extricate himself from his father's giant shadow led Michael through the gas station/hot rod days in search of a separate identity which he never quite grasped. His problems were amplified by his physical resemblance to his dad (Joel looks more like Diana) and his position as first son and namesake. Later, when his career began to take off, Michael's comments on his father and their relationship held tinges of bitterness, partially inspired by the burdens of his birthright. When asked about his famous father, Michael said, 'He's got a Beverly Hills mansion with a big fence around it – and around himself too. He drove so hard to get where he's at that it turned people off. He never learned how to take it easy . . . I never want to become that way.' And then, as always, the quick qualification, 'I'm not being critical, I merely want to make clear the difference . . . I don't come off with the toughness of my father, but I do have the same amount of drive.'

Michael's turbulent familial emotions are understandable, and his admission/denial pattern clarifies the pain he must have felt as well as the guilt. Something had gone wrong, and even though, as he's said, he knew he was loved, he needed support of a different kind. Like a lot of his generation, he found it in the extended family of the commune. As much as Kirk detested the 'squalor' his eldest willingly and enthusiastically abided in, in the long run he probably understands its final and positive effect on Michael's life.

The groovy wilderness crew found a multitude of amusing

diversions up in the hills: staging Greek Dionysian plays, laying about naked in water, all the regulation counterculture metaphysical haute couture. 'We swam naked, stomped grapes and had wine festivals,' Michael recalls fondly. As Michael grows older, he sees this time surrounded by the warm and intoxicating glow of nostalgia. The commune was his platoon, his fraternity, his generation's answer to the 'old boy' network. He realised its value, in that it compensated for and eliminated some of the insecurities he'd developed in conjunction with his family situation. His parents' divorce and the odd life he led in perennial transit, emotionally and physically, between their two worlds had somehow served to alienate him from other people, with the exception of Joel. The communal experience helped Michael adjust to the rituals and rewards of forming friendships and bonds with other people, including women people. Because he had no sisters and spent many years in all-boy schools, women were mysterious creatures in Michael's pre-commune days. His 'over-indulgence' in casual sex became less of an obsession and distraction as he spent time just living around and with women his own age; he began to trust them, and regard them in a more relaxed manner.

'We had a tight little social group of about 150 people,' he told the *New York Times* in 1969. 'A lot of them were older people in their thirties or forties who had once held white-collar jobs and who had dropped out in the days of the beatniks. We smoked a lot of pot and dropped a lot of LSD. I took quite a lot of both. I liked it . . .' Michael surfaced from the murky lake of his blissed-out state long enough to revive his half-asphyxiated educational pursuits, and eventually settled into an area guaranteed to raise the worst of his own self-doubts and his dad's ire. 'I was "undeclared" for a while in college, and then I had to "declare" so I "declared" English. Then in the last year and a half I slinked into acting. No big moments with angels and trumpets . . .' It all came down to a simple move. 'I joined the drama club and decided I loved acting.'

With theatre as his major, Michael began to focus his energies and move away from his hippie haven in the hills. Initially (and predictably), he sounded slightly disdainful of his recent past. 'I saw that most of those people just weren't very happy. Oh, it was pleasant enough sitting naked by a pool and cramming drugs down your throat. It felt good . . like a total sensual experience. But you weren't *doing* anything. It was like retiring at the age of 21.'

Michael Douglas continues to vacillate on the aftermath of this phase of his life, but for the most part, he seems to regard it as a fundamentally good excursion. A couple of years after his marriage, which of course is the ultimate familial security blanket, he perceived his early adulthood as rather silly and pointless. He took drugs because 'they made me feel like somebody.' When asked, 'Who?' he replied, 'What difference? A somebody.' He was temporarily ignoring the fact that the static, homogenous life in the commune resulted in boredom and a need to get out and create, and a very adult realisation that the mere trappings of rebellion do not a rebellion make. The freaky, long-haired hippie who zipped around with a 'chick' on his motorcycle, sporting a fashionable (and probably purple) velour shirt wasn't worth his weight in used incense, but the man who grew out of him is. 'Back then, reality was a stranger to me. I was all show and superficial as hell. Was I happy? Who asked? I didn't. My life had been about getting through, not making waves, being a chameleon. When I was with my mother I lived a New England prep school existence. Summers, with my father in Hollywood, life was different, so I was different. Just tell me how you wanted me to be and I was it.'

Michael Douglas's grand entrance into the dignified world of stage acting was neither grand nor dignified. He floated towards it, like a shipwreck survivor heading for the nearest buoy, but when he grabbed hold, he found the surface slippery and the going tougher than he'd imagined. 'It wasn't because I liked acting . . . I needed something to hang onto. It was painful. They had to keep a wastebasket just offstage for me to throw up in.' This paralysing stage fright didn't prevent him from bagging 'Best Actor of the Year' kudos in 1967, but the problem persisted through many performances.

As far as Kirk was concerned, the whole idea of his son following in his footsteps was absurd. His surprise at Michael's 'chosen' path resulted in an unfortunate eruption, tragically reminiscent of Herschel Danielovitch in its exterior aspects. After viewing Michael in a small part in the Shakespearean comedy *As You Like It*, Kirk rendered the abrupt verdict: 'You were *terrible*.' As he departed from the theatre, he thought he'd obliterated the kid's ridiculous theatrical notions in one fell stomp. 'I was very pleased because I thought that would bring him to his senses, and he'd just go off and be a good lawyer,' Kirk says. Sadly, he failed to heed his own wise words that 'A child can only imagine what it must be like to be a parent, and a parent ought to remember what it's like to be a child.'

When the elder Douglas realised the extent of Michael's burgeoning interest and the security it represented, Kirk quickly amended his critical assessments. His following appraisal was simple but complimentary. In 1974, the patriarch explained his emotional reservations, which resulted partially from a protective concern. 'Very few people (in general and in the motion picture business) criticise you constructively. They just want to destroy your confidence. I didn't want my boys to suffer that, and that's the reason I tried to discourage them from getting into pictures.'

Michael also took part in the so-called guerrilla theatre, a roving group of performers who would break into classes, fake a shooting, and watch as pandemonium erupted. 'Then we'd give a short speech about how that's what's happening in Vietnam, even as we're sitting here.' Though it wasn't the type of acting one received credit for, it remains a good memory for Michael, because it signalled the welding together of his professional life and his personal convictions.

In 1968, Michael scooped up a 'Best Director' citation from UC and also expanded his horizons by spending summers at the Eugene O'Neill Theater Centre, located in Waterford, Connecticut. The centre itself consisted of an impressive mansion, including an old barn, a garden, and acres of ground which trailed down to a beach on the Long Island Sound. The foundation featured a National Playwrights' Conference, and Frank Gagliano reported that the first of these events was widely supported by the townsfolk. 'The people of Waterford not only kicked in $10,000 of their own money to get the first four-day conference started (in 1965), but also housed the playwrights in their homes.' Authors came from all over America to argue with one another and preview new plays presented by a resident troupe, which Michael was not a part of. In return for some construction work on a Greek-style amphitheatre (in close proximity to the barn), Michael got a small part.

The following summer at the O'Neill Foundation, roomie Ron Cowen handed Michael the lead in his anti-war play, *Summertree*, which proud papa Kirk subsequently purchased the rights to. When the play landed a showcase at the Lincoln Center in New York City, Michael had a chance of taking the lead again, but he harboured reservations due to the possible effects that a leave from university might have on his draft status. Michael needn't have worried about the draft; a couple of AWOL vertebrae classified him as I-Y, though he admits his congenital handicap was overemphasised for obvious purposes. Michael managed to work out a compromise, a semester-long leave of absence, but for naught, since he lost the part after a second reading.

He finally received his BA in 1968, returned to New York City, and began working with Wynn Handman at the American Place Theater. For some time, Michael was plagued with a name problem; the unions for TV and stage both had a Bostonian registree with the name Michael Douglas, so while working in those mediums, he settled for using the moniker M. K. Douglas.

Michael found a whole new support system in New York, comprised of his work and his new friends. 'The best thing about my time in New York was that I developed a lot of good friends. And it was the first time where I found myself really accomplishing something. In college, I was just irresponsible. So I gained a lot of self-esteem working in New York. And I had all three close friends: Danny [DeVito], John Guare, Michael Lessac . . . and we're all still friends. I remember it as continuing that communal spirit of '67.'

M. K. Douglas made his television debut on February 25, 1969, in a CBS Playhouse episode entitled 'The Experiment,' a ninety-minute drama detailing the traumas of two rebels battling the corporate system. 'M. K.' played Wilson Evans, 'a hippie who has a master's degree in engineering and a company recruits him and slowly he has to conform . . .'* The hippie/prodigy is very devoted to his work and live-in-love Tess Hayes, (played by Tisha Sterling, the daughter of Ann Sothern) a militant student. Wilson, a character with 'unformed principles' decides to take 'a corporate job to continue his research and Tess agrees to stay with him. Together they plan to fulfil their

*So sayeth M. K. Douglas.

own ambitions – and avoid the compromises with business pressures and the status-conscious suburb they live in.' So sayeth *TV Guide.*

The show itself brought a fair to middling response, a fate not shared by its male lead. The next day, Michael enjoyed the first taste of public figuredom, as people approached him on the subway to compliment him on his performance. 'It was amazing,' he told Kathleen Carroll. 'I was doing a play, off-Broadway, and when I was riding to work that day in the subway people kept coming up to me and saying, "I saw you last night." ' But the professional accolades were perhaps the finest fruits harvested from his national debut. Though comparisons to Daddy-O proved inevitable, the ones expressed didn't detract from M. K.'s thunder. One critic cited the performance prophetically, 'The younger Mr Douglas could easily go as far as his father.'

The younger Mr Douglas was about to take his first step towards fulfilling this prediction by breaking onto the big screen in his first starring role . . . but personal success lagged behind the first hint of public success.

So began a rather trying period in which Michael slowly adjusted to achieving his own identity in a world which may have seemed dominated by his father, a problem similar to the ones faced by his mother many years before. He expressed interest in doing a movie with Kirk, though not a typical 'father/son story-line' film, but eventually gave up on the idea for the time being. 'The more I think of it, the more I feel it would be a difficult idea to work out. They'd tend to interpret it as cashing in on my dad's name.'

Kirk had his own worries and woes concerned with his sons and their thespian/movie biz careers. 'I worry whether my career places too much of a burden on my children. A parent's responsibility is to help a child function and find expression as a person. Functioning and finding expression sometimes comes hard to the children of so-called celebrities. They find themselves with a built-in handicap when they try to attain their own identity.'

Chapter Three

VIETNAM BLUES AND BEYOND

'I guess the sons of famous fathers are late bloomers. I know the sons of film stars who committed suicide . . . I consider myself fortunate.'

– Michael Douglas, '79

'I think having a famous father was a pain in the ass for him.'

– Kirk Douglas, '79

At the tender age of ten, Michael's awakening cinematic savvy made the newspapers, courtesy of his father and UPI. 'Those kids are something,' Kirk proudly pronounced after a couple of days spent playing basketball and baseball with Michael and Joel. 'They really keep me stepping. They're just beginning to be impressed with me as an actor, but they still kid me about the mushy scenes. They call it sissy stuff. You can't put anything over on them, particularly Mike.

'He was talking to me about a picture I'd made. He said one of the other actors was supposed to be wakened from a sound sleep by a bright light shining in his face. Mike said the actor didn't play it realistically because he didn't even squint or blink his eyes like anybody would waking up with a light like that shining in his face.'

A decade and a half later in 1969, Michael Douglas and his televised/stagebound alter ego M. K. resided in a ninety-dollar-a-month studio apartment on West Eighty-ninth Street in New York City. Within nine months of his graduation from college, Michael had scored big; he'd completed his first motion picture, *Hail, Hero!*, which premiered on October 7 at the Cheri I in Boston.

'When I read the script I flipped out,' Michael enthused in the *Sunday News*. His father's reaction was somewhat less effusive but equally ardent. The *Daily News* reported: 'Kirk was recovering from a minor throat operation when informed that the boy had landed the lead in his first movie and scribbled his reaction on a pad. "I'm speechless!" '

The screenplay scribes of *Hail, Hero!* might have profited by adopting a similar approach. Unfortunately, Michael Douglas debuted in this rank little film, which bloated to the bursting point with gabby antiwar rhetoric flying back and forth between a hip dove and his hawk parent. Unimpressive in multitudinous ways, it remains significant (and in late-late night circulation) almost solely because of its status as Michael's first starring vehicle.

Hail, Hero!'s overall mediocrity is rather surprising, considering the results director David Miller achieved when he worked with Kirk Douglas on *Lonely Are the Brave*, an excellent film containing what Kirk considers his finest performance. Whatever factors contributed to the failure of *Hail, Hero!*, it is apparent that one significant element is its leading man's inexperience. Michael would pay for his overeager, blind rush, but much to his credit, he also learned his lessons very quickly.

Other elements of Michael's first months as a 'film star' are more surprising, if one views them from a completely logistic standpoint. It seems that Michael, puffed up with youthful enthusiasm tinged with a degree of arrogance, forgot the old WW II/Hollywood words of wisdom, 'Loose lips sink ships.' With the example of Kirk (possessor of one of the looser sets of lips in the business) to remind him of the possible folly inherent in expressing oneself too freely literally hanging over his shoulder, Michael obliviously hopped into the trap awaiting many debutante celebs. Michael talked too much; not to the extent that most do when first confronted by the flattering lure of a sympathetic ear on a fishing expedition, but too much all the same. Again, to his credit, he managed to revise his approach radically after relatively few verbal faux pas.

For instance, Michael pushed even the most elastic boundaries of the public's capacity to believe when he insisted that any previous contact with David Miller 'had nothing to do with my getting the part . . . Miller didn't even *know* me when I walked in to test for the part.' Even those who weren't aware that Michael cut his professional teeth in the editing room of *Lonely Are the Brave* might experience trouble swallowing this outright denial, whether it is true or not.

Concerning other 'related' issues, Michael displayed an inordinant and almost extraordinary amount of good sense when discussing his relationship with his father. His self-control, in all but a few instances, foiled most media attempts to exploit any of the personal tensions existing between the two generations of Douglas men. In other areas, he wasn't so discreet. His frank disclosures about his sex life in particular (these were the free and easy Sixties after all) would return to haunt him via tabloids, and his tendency to be outspoken when dealing with the two big no-nos, religion and politics, must have produced some discomforting repercussions, for his tone altered significantly over the next couple of years.

Particularly politics. Michael's comments on religion were

few and far between. He once explained that Dad was Jewish, Mom wasn't, and that he hadn't been bar mitzvahed but had gotten ill at his cousin's post-ceremony celebration from overeating. Nothing exciting or shocking there, but his prelude to this simple info was a statement attesting to the fact that he felt himself 'becoming more and more Jewish,' which he attributed to an example set by blacks' examination of their heritage and a national search for identity, thereby opening himself up to three 'dangerous' topics. If the reporter had been inclined towards a certain type of journalism, Michael would have been a sitting duck for any amount of innuendo.

Another noteworthy aspect of this fundamental period also concerned Michael's public presentation of himself and the media's part in it. In spite of his occasional brashness, his somewhat guileless openness, and the potential of being labelled a showbiz bratling sailing on Daddy's coat-tails, a significant number of interviewers seemed to genuinely *like* Michael Douglas. Even when he succumbed to silly bloopers like name dropping (such as referring to Dustin Hoffman as 'Dustin'), he didn't often alienate whomever he was speaking to. It sounds absurd, but Michael's 'nice guy' status became so firmly a mainstay of his persona that he found himself in the ridiculous position of denying it in later years, insisting that he could be as much of a hard nut as anyone else in the business. But whether he liked it or not, the seeds of this peculiar predicament were planted even in the most 'rebellious' phase. There was no avoiding it – Michael possessed his own brand of charm, and even when he tried to act nonchalant or terse, a lot of people still liked him. His main satisfaction in all this may have been its diametric opposition to his father's on screen/off screen image as the charming bastard who once captured the title of 'Most Hated Man in Hollywood' in a magazine poll.

By 1971, Michael hadn't aged more than two years physically, but his mental progression was marked. He wouldn't talk about *Hail, Hero!* for the most part, and when he did his assessment balanced cagily between honesty and secrecy. Once, while weighing the pros and cons of his position as offspring of a superstar, he allowed, 'I'll even say [in] my first picture . . . maybe I was slightly exploited.'

Michael fared better with his second big screen venture, *Adam at 6 A.M.* which followed right on the heels of *Hail, Hero!* In spite of his debut effort's artistic and commercial inadequacies, something in Douglas's performance struck a responsive chord in the powers that be, and the young actor found himself spirited away to the distant realms of Orrick, Missouri, for location shooting.

The story centred around this unlikely spot partially because Elinor Karpf, who collaborated on the screenplay with her husband, came from neighbouring town Excelsior Springs and based the tale's surroundings and atmosphere on her easy familiarity with the area. Orrick, at the time, consisted of a rambling main street, banked by weatherworn one-storey houses and duplexes. Most of the town's five hundred residents spent their leisure time watching the film company at work, and many snagged bit parts in the movie itself. This, combined with the midwestern reality of the locale, added a convincing air which bolstered the movie's other good points.

The larger-than-life skies, so beloved by directors like Francis Ford Coppola (who used the dramatic sunsets which overwhelmed the industrial realities of Tulsa, Oklahoma, in his teen-epic *The Outsiders* as both an allegory and a backdrop) and the flat landscape provided a canvas for the character-centred storyline. Douglas plays a freshly hatched, counterculturesque college prof, who leaves the so-called civilisation of California to work his way through summer vacation as a 'common' labourer in Missouri.

Adam at 6 A.M. is less dated than Douglas's previous effort, and a better overall picture. Leonard Maltin's *TV Movies and Video Guide* gave it three stars (as opposed to *Hero's* one and a half, and on a scale of four stars tops to BOMB . . . the equivalent of a one-star rating), citing it as an 'underrated' venture with 'authentic location footage and good performances by [Lee] Purcell and [Joe Don] Baker' which gives it a 'rare, genuine feeling for the Midwest.' Michael's performance in this instance went unmentioned, for he still suffered from a lack of expertise which resulted in failure to make much of an impression one way or another in general. However, the film was a definite step forward in terms of its content and quality, and Michael's performance is competent if uninspiring.

Feelings on location appeared to be calm, steady, and comfortable. The filming process utilised a gigantic bus, designed by Fouad Said and valued at approximately $250,000. It could tote fifty people and their equipment comfortably, and its presence eliminated many on-location hassles which previously inconvenienced casts and crews.

Michael himself appeared stable when he faced members of the press during a breakfast conference. He commented about his work in general, 'I don't think anybody is completely satisfied . . . If you are completely satisfied, you have stopped living.' Co-producer Rick Rosenberg exclaimed that Michael 'has so much more authority [in the new film]. He has grown so much.'

Summertree changed Michael's life, not so much professionally as personally. It all started out rather innocently. 'My father, in his good Jewish mind, decided to do something for his son, put him in a movie . . . big. I had played the part in Ron Cowen's original play when it was tried out in Waterford, Connecticut, at the Eugene O'Neill. . . . My father then decided to star me in a movie of the play. Well, the thing has dragged on for years. Meanwhile, I've gotten two movies of my own.' Michael preceded these fond admissions by saying, 'Being Kirk Douglas's son can't hurt an acting career . . . It can't make you a star, either.' He was right.

This Kirk Douglas production dwells in the realm of the so-so in almost every particle of its dated body and soul. The plot line concerns yet another earnest young man trying to hash out parental differences on the metaphysical battleground of the Vietnam War. Support from experienced actors like Jack Warden and Barbara Bel Geddes couldn't quite rescue this direly distressful vehicle, possibly because the original play suffered from an overabundant distribution of crit laurels which it couldn't quite support initially, even on a small scale. The merits of the play aside, as a feature-length film it functioned not; varied receptions evened out to a lukewarm puddle.

The most monumental aspect of *Summertree*, in respect to Michael Douglas's personal history, was his introduction to co-star Brenda Vaccaro, who became his only public long-term romantic partner before he and Diandra married. In spite of a slight age difference,* Michael and Brenda shared some similarities in background. Her father was a self-made Italian immigrant and her mother a part-time actress. She originated from the East Coast, and after the family relocated to Texas she attended (for a short time) the preppy institution, Hockaday. Besides these minor similarities, kinship solidified through their mutual involvement in acting; although Brenda's list of credits far surpassed Michael's and her long climb to artistic prosperity more resembled that of his father, having traversed every medium from a bare beginning modelling swimsuits to the heady heights of international recognition as the dusky-voiced

*Brenda was born in November, 1939.

mink-coated rich woman in the late Sixties classic, *Midnight Cowboy*.

Michael has trouble explaining exactly how he and Brenda came together, other than to state vaguely that it just happened slowly during the course of filming together. Eventually they decided to take up residence together, a situation which hadn't yet gained acceptance with the general public. Regardless of fan-mag gossip, Michael and Brenda made no attempts to conceal the particulars of their relationship. In any case, Brenda already counted one ex-husband among her past loves, and she didn't feel obliged to marry just to conform to an outmoded aspect of stereotypical Hollywood morality. 'She doesn't feel any need to get married, and I share that view completely,' Michael stated in the New York Sunday *News* in 1971. 'In the old days, a woman was trapped in the cliché of "getting her man". Today, she doesn't have to feel that way and her life, hopefully, becomes richer and fuller. She didn't have the immediate necessity of getting married hanging over her head. There are other things in her life.'

As the Douglas-Vaccaro duo began to grow accustomed to each other's faces and bathroom habits, they also instituted a somewhat footloose existence, moving from West Coast to East Coast, visiting Europe, and spending time on Michael's hundred-plus acres near Grafton, Vermont, in a forty-foot trailer.

After years of running free and wild, Michael settled down and focused his energy, in his personal and professional life. Though tabloids still carried hints of Kirk's supposed displeasure, the elder Douglas took pains to be positive about Michael and Brenda's decision. 'Everybody should live together. It's better than rushing into marriage,' he told *Interview* magazine in 1974. Perhaps unconsciously countering the archaic vision of cohabiting couples as sexual desperados who avoided marriage for the purpose of Olympian screw-fests and other rampantly unmonogamous activities, Kirk went on to say, 'Michael has gotten less promiscuous . . . he's been with a lot of different girls, but he's settled down with Brenda. I think she's terrific.' He continued to reiterate that he supported and approved of their living arrangement, and offered this story to underline the old 'wed in haste, repent in leisure' theory. 'My son Joel was going with a girl and wanted to get married. So I said, why don't you two just live together for a while . . .' According to Kirk, Joel didn't heed his father's advice. 'He got married and now he's divorced,' Kirk concluded.

Meanwhile, Brenda and Michael, far from indulging in whatever paganistic pursuits others envisioned for them, became so happily dug in that they were three skips short of boring. Besides their travels, they both had careers to attend to. Brenda was making the rounds stage-wise and continuing to pursue guest roles on television shows like *The Name of the Game*, and Michael gained a coveted accolade and a hitherto-lacking aura of legitimacy for his portrayal of 'Jerry the Naz' in an acclaimed off-Broadway play called *Pinkville*.

Pinkville ran for six weeks at the American Place Theater, close to Times Square and the regular Broadway circles. The atmosphere encouraged Michael in his return to the stage, for the American Place, like other off-Broadway venues, operated on a subscription basis. 'You know you'll be playing to a full house for a specified time,' he said in *Women's Wear Daily*. 'Unlike Broadway a critic can't close the show after one night.'

Michael portrayed a freshly recruited Marine from Queens, New York, who arrives at his boot camp with a Bible in one hand and a strong moral conviction to uphold the 'Thou shalt not kill' commandment in his heart. Browbeaten into psychological surrender by a sadistic superior, he leaves for Vietnam, ready to kill anything which gets in his way. The theatre itself contributed to the intensity of the play with its 'in the round' set up. 'I like it that way,' Michael affirmed. 'It's more intimate, but it also requires great concentration. You can hear every little noise.' The only aspect of the presentation he found personally discomforting involved the requirement that he stay onstage before the play actually started. 'I'd rather be conserving my strength backstage. It's hard to sit out there and see your friends in the audience.'

The play used music to convey some of its ideas, and, yes, Michael did quite a bit of singing. 'It's not like a musical. The songs have no big introduction. They make a point which might otherwise be too tedious if it is made by a speech. You don't get the feeling you're being hit over the head with it.'

Pinkville appeared at a time when questioning the war was no longer the private property of the so-called lunatic fringe. Lieutenant Calley's Hun-like massacre put the tiny town of My Lai on everyone's lips, and his trial ran simultaneously with the play. '*Pinkville* is a fair portrayal of the harassment that goes on during training. It's the story of a good boy who is made a killer . . . how he succumbs to the machine. When asked about the real-life parallels of My Lai, Michael responded, 'The blame lies in the philosophy of the training, where one gets his attitude.'

Critical and public response united to praise Michael's part and the musical/play itself. Later, he and Brenda gained another shared experience when he won the Theatre World Award. (She had captured it almost ten years earlier.)

'The first time I met Michael,' Karl Malden recalls, 'I was coming in to try on some clothes for Quinn Martin. Quinn introduced him. I said "Kirk's son? That's good enough . . ." '

Michael had finished an *FBI* episode for the busy producer, replacing another actor at the last minute in 'The Hitchhiker.'

Michael's more-than-decent performance as a gun-toting thief suffered from a brief case of overexposure. After Michael's initial frenzied entrance, he returned to ask the director about his scene, content that he'd effected a flabbergasted response from the 'patrons.' 'I came back to ask the director how it was and he said, "Well, take a look . . ." My fly was open. So the shocked expression when everybody looked . . . they didn't know if I was a bank robber or a pervert.'

After this rousing start, Michael's agency began pushing him towards a new Quinn Martin production called 'The Streets of San Francisco'. Michael reacted initially to the TV stigma, an off-the-books professional code which classified actors much more stringently at the time. However, the offer came when nothing else, especially juicy movie roles, was in evidence, and Michael found himself at an awkward age, acting-wise . . . too old to be Joe College, too young to be Joe Leading Man. As it turned out, taking on the part of Steve Keller worked excellently for Michael and everyone else involved.

One beneficial facet of Michael's stint on television came from his association with Academy Award winner Karl Malden. The two got on famously, and both never hesitated to heap praise upon each other, and the whole crew in general. Years later Michael still remembers his days on location in San Francisco fondly: 'That was a great experience. We did fifty-two minutes of finished film in seven shooting days. Karl and I would finish a scene, grab the film cans and camera, hop into the truck and go off to another location. It taught me a very valuable lesson about filmmaking. If a show is going to work out, everyone – cast and crew – has to work together.'

As for Mr Malden himself, he impressed Michael deeply with his professionalism and skill. 'Even though I was comparatively new to the business, Karl never gave me the feeling I was a beginner. Another star would perhaps have felt the threat of rivalry and tried to push me into the background . . . perhaps it's because he knew my father from earlier days and played with him on the stage, but Karl is rather protective towards me, almost as if I were his son. Karl has already won an Oscar but he still takes the trouble to talk things over with me and helps me from taking the back seat.'

Initially, the 'back seat' got a bit uncomfortable, and Michael and the show took a while to find their places. Michael registered some uneasiness after his first season in the prime-time lane; Steve Keller wasn't sufficiently defined, and the show wasn't in the optimum slot. He remembers, 'Back in my father's day there was a normal progression for an actor's career. He could get his start on Broadway then a studio would take him over and mould his career.'

'But when I went to New York in '68, there was no theatre. I did a little off-Broadway, then I made two or three pictures that didn't go. The studios don't put actors under contract any more so I figured the best way to move my career along was to get into a TV series.'

After the Nielsen disappointment of the first season, things evened out to everyone's advantage. 'During that period I seemed to be taking one step forward and two steps back. I finally told Quinn that I wanted out unless I had more to do. He was understanding and it has worked out so I have a show, Karl has a show, then we do one together. It's good for us, and good for the series.'

'The Streets of San Francisco' is certainly nothing to be ashamed of, and Michael is fortunate to have been connected with a quality production during this crucial time in his career. He played Assistant Inspector Steve Keller, college graduate, the youngest of his rank in the San Francisco Police Department, and partner of street-smart old hand Mike Stone (Karl Malden). The two formed a super-successful team who triumphed over the forces of crime for four seasons, earning Michael three Emmy nominations in the process.

Cop shows were really hip during the early seventies, and a consistently good show with stunning locations and a broad-based appeal like 'Streets' equalled money in the bank, and for Michael the type of recognition he desired via a medium as yet unconquered by his father. Kirk, while mourning the passage of the western as a popular genre, said: 'I guess there were too many for a long while. . . . Today, everyone's a policeman, including my son Michael. He's been in ['San Francisco'] for three years . . . living it up in this beautiful city in a penthouse overlooking the bay. . . . His poor old father has been stuck out in the desert with dust, flies, and horse manure.* I think a policeman's life beats a cowboy's every time.'

During his stint in San Fran, Michael spent as much time with Brenda as possible, but with a six-day-a-week working schedule the situation wasn't exactly smooth, and maintaining their calm life began to require a more flexible attitude and a proclivity for rapid transport. Brenda didn't want to move from LA, where they inhabited a large house in Benedict Canyon, for fear that a permanent relocation to San Fran would damage her career. Besides, the city itself didn't agree with her. 'I'd die there. You've gotta climb hills; groceries have to be delivered,' and in any case, 'I find it kind of provincial.' Nonetheless, Brenda visited Michael and vice versa, and the couple insisted on the solidity of their union. 'We've been together for four years,' Michael proudly exclaimed. 'That's longer than half the marriages here.' Brenda added, 'I lived with a guy for two years and was married to him for three. I was made to feel more responsible after we were married . . . another contract. It should be a spiritual thing. When you're married you try

*Kirk had recently completed a kind of political allegory western called *Posse*, a well-made effort which was ignored for the most part by audiences.

harder. Who needs that kind of pressure?' Michael concluded, 'Neither of us is against marriage, but we're happy the way it is. Nobody says to me "You can't have it because you're not married." '

Regardless of the dislocating factors of Michael's seasonal migrations northward, the Douglas-Vaccaro lifestyle during his time off hadn't changed much from early days in New York, when Michael stated, 'We hardly go out at all. We watch a lot of television. I myself am interested in sports on TV, the only live drama left on the medium.' (Such admissions conjure up images of, 'Bring me another beer honey (belch).') In California, their life was a bit more diverse but hardly shockingly unusual. Michael and Brenda would rent a Cessna and fly to Santa Barbara or Catalina for the weekend (he'd got his pilot's licence) or indulge in another hobby, photography, or just spend hours lolling around on the beach.

Michael and Brenda didn't spent time entertaining business types, preferring intimate dinners at home with close friends. 'They all know the Broadway musicals and we often stage our own rendition right here in the living room.' Sometimes they'd venture out to a movie or the theatre, and dinners out with friends shifted between Italian, Japanese, and Mexican. More importantly, 'Helping each other is what we spend the most time doing. If you're not doing that in a relationship, you better get out.' Michael later mentioned a notion circulating among their close friends of forming a slightly more polite, classy version of the communal structure he'd inhabited in his untamed youth, perhaps this time in an expansive house with some sort of central area. He'd begun to hanker for his old support group. 'My life was a lot simpler then,' he sighed, going on to lament the complications of growing older and dealing with an increasingly busy career, but he insisted the main goal in his life was to achieve a balance between his personal and professional lives ... something which would become increasingly difficult.

In contrast, life on the 'Streets' could be rather frantic and exciting. Michael took some sailing lessons in the bay, and smashed up a Lotus during a short foray into sports-car racing. Malden's stand-in attested to his prowess behind the wheel, and Douglas cheerfully related the particulars of a car chase from the pilot. 'I whipped the car around a corner and over one of those San Francisco hills and it seemed like all four wheels left the ground. Karl and I were both airborne. I looked over at him and he looked at me and said, "This is going to be an *interesting* series." '

In late '74, Michael performed a less frivolous feat when he saved a stunt man named Robert Butler who was accidentally mowed down by a powerboat during filming. 'The water all around him was turning red. The next thing I knew, I was in the water – fully clothed – swimming towards him. It was just an instinctive reaction on my part.' Butler replied, 'Without Mike's prompt action I'm sure I'd never have made it. I'll be forever grateful to him for saving my life.' Michael received a Presidential citation for his bravery.

By the series' third season, Karl Malden told the *TV Times*, 'The relationship of Mike and Steve – the old cop and the young one, the kidding around, the generation gap, which I think is one of the genuine strengths of the show – is the way I am with Mike Douglas. If Mike Stone treats Steve with more respect now, because he's matured as a cop, I treat Mike Douglas with the same respect because he has really matured as an actor.' He also cited the show's increasingly diverse plots, good critical and audience reaction, and lovely background they shot within. 'There are three stars of the series: Mike Douglas and me and San Francisco.'

Everyone predicted a fine future for the eldest Douglas offspring, who through the miracle of television was quickly becoming as familiar to the public as his old man. Kirk happily told Michael of an instance when a woman approached him for an autograph and then blurted out, 'Oh thank you, Mr Douglas. My daughter will be so pleased. She's a great fan of your son's!'

Quinn Martin commented, 'Michael's got the potential to have a great future. When he's through with the series he'll be mature enough to get feature roles. He's been a great asset to us, and will be to anyone.' Yes, everyone held high hopes for Michael Douglas's acting career, meanwhile disregarding an outside, personal project which he'd been carrying on his shoulders along with the burdens of a weekly television role . . . a little independent something called *One Flew Over the Cuckoo's Nest.*

Chapter Four

A CUCKOO'S NEST

'Well, if he isn't proud now, I don't think he ever will be. He has seen both the success and failure of the sons and daughters of his friends, and there are as many successes as failures.'

– Michael Douglas '78

'If a film is well made, why shouldn't it, like a good book or painting, be valid for the next generation?'

– Kirk Douglas '78

'These kids keep shoving . . . and shoving . . . and pretty soon they push the old-timers right off.'

– Kirk Douglas '59

'Douglas says he will make more money from the picture his son produced than he has from any of his own films.'

– *Daily News* '76

The saga of the Douglas family's involvement with *One Flew Over the Cuckoo's Nest* spanned generations and decades. It also signalled the beginning of a family tradition as Kirk passed on his penchant for entanglement in confusing and complex business shenanigans to his two oldest sons. Soon Michael and Joel were linked to their father and his 'other' family by blood, sweat, deals galore, and a magnificent film crowned with five Oscars, which grossed over $200 million.

In the beginning, there was Kirk. He bought the rights to Ken Kesey's novel soon after its publication in 1962, intending to translate the burgeoning cult favourite into an artistic and commercial Broadway success. His passionate commitment to the story and its enticing main character, Randall P. McMurphy, led to his first stage appearance since the *Woman Bites Dog* folly of 1947. With Dale Wasserman authoring a stage version, Kirk enthused over the project despite the loud voices of nay-sayers insisting that his place was on screen.

After forty-one films and seventeen years, Kirk opened his play in New Haven at the Shubert Theater.* Theatre critic John Molleson, in attendance at a New Haven matinee, noted a plethora of squealing, autograph-hunting teeny-boppers (of the female variety) waiting outside the Shubert, a vehement reminder of Kirk's screen-idol status. During their subsequent interview, Douglas confided his hopes for a long run at the Cort Theater on Broadway before taking the project to Hollywood for transferral to film mode. He also confessed to his initial nervous apprehension concerning the play.

With opening night behind him and the assurance of various friends, co-stars, and the director to bolster his unstable sense of command, Kirk gradually eased himself into the rhythm of the play and his performance. He explained his mixed feelings and the broad spectrum of emotions encompassed in his recurring attraction to the footlights in a simple allegory: 'It's a compulsion with me. It's the kid who's frightened of the graveyard forcing himself to go there in the middle of the night.'

*Across the street, the Robert Sherman cinema marquee advertised *20,000 Leagues Under the Sea*.

By most accounts, Kirk's portrayal of McMurphy and the play itself were exciting and sensational. Douglas entered the project prepared to forgo Tinseltown's monetary bonbons for at least four months. 'I felt that with a cast of more than twenty actors I owed it to all to stay for the whole season – to be fair to the group,' he told John Molleson. He found the part stimulating, with its balance of psychosis, tragedy, and humour.

Sadly, the Broadway run failed to break any box-office records and when Kirk attempted production of a film version,* he encountered apathetic disinterest. 'No studio would take a chance on doing it,' he told the Syracuse *New Times*. 'Why, I never knew. I never thought of it as an arty film. It was a brilliant story, just on sheer dramatic value. After a while, I got beaten down. You're fighting the system, but it's like the guy in *Lonely Are the Brave*: You keep on fighting the system and you're going to get destroyed.'

A lawsuit from Dale Wassserman plus various other disconcerting difficulties intervened. Kirk felt the role slipping away as he grew older; in his eyes, he could no longer portray McMurphy effectively . . . not at his age. *Cuckoo's Nest*, the movie, entered the dead files for a few years. Meanwhile, the book and Dale Wasserman's play continued to make the rounds and gain popularity.

Michael harboured no secret desire to produce, but his father's effort to sell his *Cuckoo's Nest* rights in 1970** spurred him into action. His feelings for the book mirrored Kirk's sentiments; he loved it and couldn't understand why it wasn't movie material. If he'd known that *Cuckoo's Nest* would take five years of wheeling and dealing to bring to the screen, he might have run for the hills.

*In which he hoped to feature Gene Wilder and William Daniels, both veterans of the Broadway version.

**For $150,000.

The tale that the Douglases found so intriguing is a riveting composite of allegory, fable, action, and social commentary. Its parade of very three-dimensional characters orbits around Randall P. McMurphy and Nurse Ratched, who are locked in a struggle to the death.

McMurphy, a convict, fakes insanity to achieve a transfer from the harshness of prison to the relatively 'cushy' life of the state mental hospital. Once inside, he becomes involved with the other patients, administering his own type of care. This challenge to order and authority incenses Nurse Ratched, the villainess in white who leads to his downfall.

While simultaneously co-starring on 'The Streets of San Francisco' and rushing off to production meetings, Michael took advantage of his visibility to plug his picture. In an interview with the *Los Angeles Times*, he lavished praise on the book and his father's commitment to *Cuckoo's Nest*. 'My old man thought so much of that book that he left movies to go back to Broadway for the first time in eighteen years,' Michael asserted proudly (perhaps momentarily forgetting that his dad *wanted* to go back to Broadway more than just about anything). 'The play was no great hit – it ran about eight months. But it's been playing somewhere ever since. There's a San Francisco production that's been running for five years.'

'Dad tied up the rights to the movie but nobody in Hollywood was interested. "Who wants to laugh at crazy people?" they asked him . . .'

With the majors' renewed disinterest paining the pride and posterior of a second generation of Douglases, Michael pulled a 'Kirk' and snubbed the establishment. He sought financing elsewhere, among his own contemporaries, and struck a gusher when he hooked up with Saul Zaentz of Berkeley's Fantasy Records (home of Creedence Clearwater Revival, et al.). Zaentz proved sympathetic to the unusual premise of the novel and attuned to its possibilities; he pledged his support as co-producer and major financier.*

Michael found his schedule filling to the bursting point as he dashed madly between his two main interests. An average day on 'The Streets of San Francisco' consumed fourteen hours, and a 'day off' constituted zipping across the bridge to meet with Saul Zaentz in Berkeley and attending to such diverse matters as money, casting, and the exasperations caused by initial endeavours to pull together a screenplay.

With the film rights in their pockets and sufficient financing, Zaentz and Douglas contacted Ken Kesey. According to Michael, Zaentz wanted to assign Kesey the screenplay and get him 'in on' the picture, even though there were no legal responsibilities or reasons for doing so. The three met, and Zaentz told Kesey that he'd get a piece of the action even if he didn't write the screenplay; but if he did, he'd receive an additional salary.

Kesey composed a bizarre rendition of his own book. In one scene a nurse sporting a 'Vulcarian' helmet scratches the walls, producing streams of blood à la Polanski. Michael and Saul continued to hope, and requested rewrites, but Kesey suddenly reappeared with an agent and a list of demands. Everything stalled and, in the end, Kesey was out.** Michael still liked the book, but his idealised vision of Ken Kesey, eccentric genius, had dimmed somewhat.

As per selection of the movie's director, father and son coincidentally targetted the same man for their pet project at wholly separate times. Kirk encountered Mr Forman during a trip to Czechoslovakia and mailed him a copy of the book for his perusal. Receiving no reply, Kirk assumed that Forman wasn't interested; but actually the package never reached its

*Mr Zaentz invested about $2 million in *Nest*.

**This is the gospel according to Michael, as told to *Rolling Stone*.

intended. When Michael informed Kirk of his chosen director for *Cuckoo's Nest*, the elder Douglas was literally floored.

Continuing legal entanglements with Wasserman further hindered the younger Douglas's attempts to get the ball rolling. 'We were ready to go a year ago but the rights were snarled in litigation,' Michael explained. 'We want to do the book, not the play. That's cleared now.'

Some aspects of the delay were fortuitous: 'It took a couple of years to make the deal. By then I had had some production experience, having worked on "Streets" for four years. I only acted in the show . . . but when you are an integral part of the making of a one-hour film every six days for four years, you can't help but notice how films are made. So that served me well,' Michael told Gene Siskel of the Chicago *Tribune* in 1979.

In their search for the perfect McMurphy, Michael and Milos Forman skimmed through a veritable Who's Who of Hollywood actors. Gene Hackman passed, as did Marlon Brando. Forman proposed an offbeat choice, Burt Reynolds, but Reynolds wasn't interested.

Miscellaneous commitments and extenuating circumstances delayed casting long enough to allow Jack Nicholson to accept the McMurphy role. 'Everything seems to be working out perfectly,' enthused Michael. 'We'll wind up our season* about the time Nicholson completes the new Mike Nichols film (*The Fortune*). Some of this great crew of "Streets of San Francisco" will go to Oregon to work on the film.'

The 'vibes' on location in Oregon were good; the crew and cast of *Cuckoo's Nest* were probably the first people to have a blast in the Oregon State Mental Hospital in Salem. Nicholson's arrival preceded general admittance, allowing him to spend a couple of weeks at the hospital in preparation for

*On 'Streets.'

filming. Jack's reputation as a hard worker inclined to adopting, or rather, swallowing up his roles is well deserved, and the complex character of Randall P. McMurphy required whole-hearted devotion and attention.

'I don't quite have McMurphy down yet,' he said to a fellow cast member after they'd commenced shooting. 'I'm still playing my own quality. I could name you five guys in Hollywood who are more right for this part than I am. I wasn't sure it was right for me, but I loved the book so much I took it.'

Soon Mr Nicholson's doubts evaporated and his playful nature bubbled to the surface, merging with similar qualities which made McMurphy endearing. Jack and various friends (including his 'steady,' Anjelica Huston) made nightly forays into the nearest town in search of adventure, driving Nicholson's Mercedes 600 (which featured a bar in the back), and raising Cain.

At other times, Nicholson kicked back and let go of his character. He passed time on the set playing pinball; just another actor killing time between takes. Once, in a gesture reminiscent of McMurphy's generous side, he threw a birthday party for a hospital inmate.

Decorative laurels of critical approval were bestowed upon Mr Nicholson, above and beyond his previous lion's share. Additionally, he received notice for the professionalism, generosity, and sense of balance he maintained with the rest of the cast, for without the lead character's graceful cooperation, an ensemble piece like *Cuckoo's Nest* is doomed.

Charles Champlin of the *Los Angeles Times* reported, 'The novel, a continuing best seller, became a frequently produced play and has now become one of the year's best-made and most engrossing movies, offering still another dimension of Jack Nicholson's phenomenal powers as an actor. . . . The acting honours are shared by Nicholson with a large and almost totally unfamiliar, but meticulously well chosen supporting cast. He and they constitute an ensemble whose quality is such that they always seem characters colliding and never actors acting.'

An alliance solidified on the set of *Cuckoo's Nest*: Messrs Douglas and Nicholson embarked on one of the longest boys'-nights-out in recent history (and a somewhat notorious one at that). When Michael and Jack first met, they established an immediate rapport. Nicholson's reputation and growing status surrounded him with an aura of unreality, but Michael and he quickly disposed of the goat-godlike image and got down to basics. In the end, they were just two guys who shared a love for movies, the experiences of their generation, and a wicked, slightly sick sense of humour.

This partnership was destined to lead to all sorts of wild goings-on, some possibly too scandalous for public consumption. Both Jack and Mike are inclined to clam up when queried on their escapades. One shouldn't assume the worst on the basis of their silence and smirks; it could be a case of allowing the public's collective imagination to fester and cultivate impossible horrors nobody is capable of. Or one can assess the possible excess by what Michael *would* reveal:

'When we were shooting *Cuckoo's Nest* in Oregon, Jack Nicholson and I were invited to something they called a "Hollywood party". Curious to see what this was, we went over there and discovered it was a wife-swapping party. We stuck around and watched while they got it on. Jack and I aren't wife-swappers, but we were *major* voyeurs,' Michael laughed.

Soon, in any case, Michael wouldn't be in any position to 'wife' swap. The added strain of heading a large production while starring on 'Streets' plus dozens of other complicating factors were encroaching on the blissful union of Brenda and Michael.

When rewards for the film began pouring in, the Douglas/

Nicholson duo continued on, hell-bent-for-leather, going-to-Hades-in-a-handcart-burning-their-bridges-behind-style. Michael's break with Brenda Vaccaro freed him for whatever the world had to offer, so the actor and the producer set off on a six-week-long promotional tour encompassing Denmark, England, France, Germany, Sweden, Japan, and Australia. Nicholson jumped ship, and Michael continued on to Brazil, Mexico, Venezuela and other exotic South American ports of call.

In late 1974, after finishing a supporting role in the legendary flop *Once Is Not Enough* with Kirk Douglas,* Brenda Vaccaro made some of her most candid admissions concerning her relationship with Michael to journalist Joyce Haber. 'I believe in risks. It's scary as hell. A safe place is necessary but risk is important. A balance between those two is an incredible way to live. Having marriage with bonds or anchors – the refrigerator, the station wagon – or having nothing are both extremes. I don't believe in either. I believe there's a middle. The middle is ecstasy. To reach it takes lots of time, because you can't do away with conditioning. It's the nature of the human being not to find the middle. So what I'm saying is that living with someone leads you to the same place. Freedom is only within yourself.'

The ultimate freedom loomed large in the couple's future, and by late 1975, they were separated for good. Michael contends that career conflicts were an important element of their split. In 1974, Michael practically admitted that his avoidance of the altar wasn't altogether an offshoot of some early Seventies, former-hippie-armchair-mellow self-discovery process when the *Enquirer* quoted him as saying, 'I was also probably frightened about getting into something I couldn't just

*In spite of the movie's overall awfulness, Ms Vaccaro outdid everyone, including Kirk, and received an Academy Award nomination for her pains.

end by walking out the door.' The article contained other quotes attesting to the couple's desire to marry and produce babies.

With a hit on his hands and plenty of money rolling in, Michael sowed his wild oats in grand fashion: 'After *Cuckoo's Nest* came out, people were always glad to see me. I went around the world promoting the picture and I enjoyed myself. I was single at the time, so I made every effort to savour the experience in the most decadent way . . . I think a few people were worried about what I was doing to myself. I got a little excessive.'

As for those unlucky companies who rejected *Cuckoo's Nest*, Michael eagerly heaped insult on their injuries: 'I'm not always a nice guy. A number of film studios turned me down on *Cuckoo's Nest*. And some of these same men also turned down *The China Syndrome*. They really **** around with me. Well, I keep tabs. I'll get even. But in the meantime, I'm getting great satisfaction.'

After *Cuckoo's Nest* and *China Syndrome* triumphed so magnificently, the press corps was naturally curious about the secret of Michael's success as a producer. 'I just don't put together a deal and walk away,' he explained to Gene Siskel. 'I stay with a production. . . . And I think I'm a pretty good sounding board for people. I never take a domineering role. Some producers like making deals. I like making movies.'

As a footnote to the whole affair, Ken Kesey surfaced in early 1976 bearing subpoenas. The novelist filed a federal court suit against the distributors, producers, and owners of *One Flew Over the Cuckoo's Nest*. Kesey entered the complaint in the US District Court in Portland, Oregon, claiming that the defendants broke an agreement which promised him a whopping five per cent of the movie's gross. In addition, he sought approximately $870,000 in damages. The defendants were Michael Douglas,

Saul Zaentz, Fantasy Products Inc., United Artists, and Skylark Filmaatschappij BV (a Dutch corporation).

With the film nominated for nine Oscars, the en masse immediate reaction of the defendants was 'no comment.' Kesey's complaint stated that he'd sold the movie rights to Kirk Douglas in '62, and those rights found their way into Skylark's possession some time after. Skylark then enlisted Zaentz as production contractor and Michael Douglas took control of production duties. Supposedly, Kesey entered into an oral agreement with Michael and Saul in 1972 to author the screenplay for five per cent of *Cuckoo's Nest*'s gross plus certain advances and additional payments for rewrites.

The defendants allegedly employed two other people for the screenplay and refused to honour or acknowledge the existence of any contract with Mr Kesey, verbal or otherwise. Mr Kesey further claimed that his approval for the use of his name in conjunction with the finished film wasn't secured.

Kesey skipped the April 1976 Oscar ceremony; he wasn't invited and he had a date to play poker. 'I'd like to have subpoenas in some of those award envelopes,' Mr Kesey commented, referring to the evasiveness of certain litigants. Kesey's rejected screenplay escaped mention as the recipients for the Best Screen adaptation collected their award.

Mr Kesey added that although he liked Jack Nicholson as an actor (he still hadn't seen the film), he would have chosen someone else for the part – Kirk Douglas.

Chapter Five

A CHANGE OF LIFE

'Michael is away for such long stretches of time. Cameron is my best friend.'

– Diandra Douglas, '84

'I just think it's healthier for Diandra and I to keep work and our marriage as separate as possible.'

– Michael Douglas, '88

'My idea of romance is that every day some little incident takes on a special meaning because of who you are sharing it with. . . . And when you have a wife who is as funny and beautiful and interesting as mine, it's not *too* difficult to be romantic.'

– Michael Douglas, '86

'They look like an S&M couple. She's wearing the dog collar. He married her for her looks and never lets her forget it.'

– Tama Janowitz, *People* magazine, '88

With one 'marriage' and two extended bouts of satyrlike bacchanalias trailing in his wake, Michael Kirk Douglas blew into Washington, DC, to celebrate Jimmy Carter's inauguration and the additional festive hoopla which surrounds such events. He and Jack Nicholson strode manfully off to Political Party Central, ready for almost anything and everything, except what lay in wait.

The night began with a Kennedy Center concert to mark Inaugural Eve, followed by a more exclusive upstairs reception with the President-to-be. Then, in a fashion either fairy tale or cornball, depending on your point of view,* Michael glanced around the room and saw *the* girl: nineteen-year-old Diandra Luker.

All of a sudden, infatuation ran up and kicked Michael square in the butt, and he never even saw it coming. For years afterwards he remained mystified and in awe as to the exact nature of this all-enveloping grand passion. What hit him is not known, but who hit him is. Diandra spent some of her childhood in Deyá, a tiny town on the sunny island of Majorca, off the coast of Spain. Her father, an American diplomat, died when she was young. Her mother is an archaeologist. She grew up among artists and other archaeologists, and saw many parts of the world via extensive travels and from behind the walls of several boarding schools. Michael and Diandra came close to crossing paths when they were both in Santa Barbara, but only relatively; he was a freshman in college and she was nine years old.

Through her years of scattered but intense schooling, Diandra mastered five languages and never had enough time to watch a lot of television. Three years previous to her entrance into Michael's life, she settled in Washington, DC, her birthplace, to study for a diplomatic career in Georgetown University's School of Foreign Service.

*Michael usually opts for 'corny.'

Ms Luker didn't know Michael from Adam. Even if she'd seen him as Steve Keller, Michael had grown a very imposing beard. Diandra imagined that behind the wall of hair a painter or sculptor lurked; Michael perceived Diandra as an ethereal creature, almost literally wrenched from a classic painting, adding fuel to the theory labelling first impressions as foolish notions. After an introduction, the twosome began tentative moves toward acquaintance. Michael's line pertained to 'the quality of the hors d'oeuvres.' Diandra labelled the resulting conversation 'ridiculous' and 'vigorous,' and intensely interesting: 'He was different. He had different perspectives about things. . . . He was Sixties, rock and roll, and drugs. I had never heard of that. We were people from opposite worlds.' When the worlds collided, Michael equally enjoyed both Diandra's old world aura and the fact that she was 'real *smart*,' a fortuitous fringe benefit which promised the potential of a longer-term romance than the kind he'd recently indulged in.

Basically, the situation quickly ran away with itself, altering Michael and Diandra's lives immediately and completely. They stayed well within reach for the remainder of their courtship, brief though it was. It seems that the somewhat apocalyptic occasion of their first physical union corresponded with Diandra's discovery of Michael's actual profession and his position in the world. 'I was shocked,' she remembers. 'But it was too late.'

Within less than two weeks, *the* question popped out of the besotted Mr Douglas. Diandra's initial surprise didn't seriously affect either her feelings or her affirmative reply. Michael later explained his sudden change of heart and a yen to settle down as an inevitable outcome of meeting Ms Right, but other elements probably contributed to his instant urge to merge.

After Michael split with Brenda, his tune changed slightly. Previously, when referring to his family's opinion of their arrangement, Michael joked and Kirk joked but neither really sprang to address the issue if it could be avoided. Later, he would say, 'With all the work I've had preparing the picture (*Cuckoo's Nest*) plus problems with the families, it got to be too much of a hassle.' It may have been a simple case of the number one son being expected to begin the next generation, or Brenda's parents putting on pressure, or a combination. In any case, evidence suggests that Michael felt the firm grip of his family's anticipations closing in on him.

This type of future with Brenda wasn't in the cards. Supposedly, a flaw in their relationship caused both to fight the idea of marriage the longer they stayed together, even though towards the end of their relationship an article would appear here or there indicating that they were considering a permanent situation and children. This quirk in an otherwise consistent public repartee indirectly supports other aspects of a romance suffering from its parties growing apart rather than together. As their relationship went into its final phase, their proclamations attesting to an utterly fabulous life sans legal bonds became overtly stringent. True, their position in the celebrity hierarchy led to repeated demands to justify their living arrangement, but as things crumbled, both Brenda and Michael began to almost *over*explain, practically as if they were compelled to convince themselves, or someone closer than the public.

Michael's talk of resuming his communal existence also bespoke a possible inner yearning for additional emotional support, since he apparently equated 'gangs' and 'groups' with a certain type of stability. Brenda confided, in the hindsight of post-split, that she'd slowly realised her feelings for Michael (and vice versa) weren't evolving in a marital direction, and consequently she became somewhat ambivalent about their relationship. Various theories, conflicting explanations, catty remarks, and zipped-lipped silences were exchanged when enquiring reporters wanted to delve into the fate of this highly visible couple. Because of so many contradictions, most of the clues to Michael's probable motivations and state of mind lie in his manic return to bachelorhood and equally enthusiastic wild rush into marital bliss. In any case, Michael and Diandra's romance subtly suggests the presence of a few ghosts remaining to haunt after his five-year relationship with Ms Vaccaro ended.

In addition, the factor of Michael's age can't be excluded from the overall picture: it's common knowledge that men entering their thirties often feel the need to reassess their lives as visions of mortality encroach, and this directly affects views of marriage and children. Michael had obviously pondered the various fundamental psychological puzzlers posed by reproductive urges; he even confided to a *Cosmopolitan* reporter that he'd entertained admittedly chauvinistic fantasies of distributing himself throughout womankind, spreading his seed about and reaping a harvest of little half-Michaels. Clearly, such notions indicate either the presence of a desire to progenate or a megalomaniacal ego. In Mr Douglas's case, taking into account his assertion that he'd received several offers from women ready and willing to bear his children, one can assume a genuine desire for a family of his own could inspire him to fling himself into a situation which formerly seemed uninviting.

On March 20, 1977, a scant two months after the inane hors d'oeuvres comments, the attractive couple wed in Kirk and Anne's Beverly Hills home. Guests included Karl Malden, Gregory Peck, Warren Beatty, and Jack Nicholson. It wasn't a humongous Hollywood free-for-all – a couple of dozen friends and relatives gathered to witness the 'bolt from the blue' union of two people very obviously in love. Nor did the wedding hold any obvious echoes of Michael's hippie roots for the bride wore a veil and gown, and the groom sported a dapper suit.

Michael and Diandra Douglas moved to LA, where Michael

hoped to continue making beautiful business and Diandra resumed her schooling at the University of California. Suddenly, she found herself enveloped by movie people, and she didn't especially enjoy the disparity between her life and those of the people her newlywed husband associated with. Diandra realised that she must seem likewise enigmatic to the citizens of Hollywood. 'Being young, I found it difficult to grow in an environment where I was always surrounded by people in one profession. It was like being surrounded by dentists for the formative years of your life,' she told the *New York Times* in 1987. Other potential trouble spots were emphasised by their locale. 'There was an experience gap,' Diandra explains. 'We were both aware that if we didn't make changes, the relationship didn't have a chance.'

After December 13, 1978, Cameron Morrell Douglas became another important consideration in the relationship. With two years in LA behind them, the threesome relocated to Santa Barbara, which they found more conducive to healthy childrearing. Diandra attended Michael's alma mater, but Michael had problems resolving and/or implementing business procedures from 'out of town,' so they eventually moved back to LA, where Diandra occupied herself by learning something about film, working on the *Los Angeles Weekly* (which Michael had a hand in starting), and involving herself in another of Michael's interests – the Committee of Concern. This group, mostly consisting of those in the entertainment industry, helped sponsor various educational events highlighting the socio-political issues of Central America. However, when Diandra continued to feel uncomfortable in LA, the Douglases began to reconsider moving back East. With Michael's continuing successes to bolster his position in the movie business, the couple felt secure enough to venture beyond the bounds of California and back to New York City.

Another important aspect in this decision was young Cameron. Michael considered himself extremely fortunate to become a father at a time when his financial security was a certainty, and he didn't feel compelled to spend every day slugging away in the salt mines. With *The China Syndrome* finished, Michael switched traditional roles with Diandra, allowing her sufficient time to continue college while he got to have a major hand in bringing up baby. 'I stayed with Cameron and was able to create a bonding which carried me through the periods when I've had to be apart from him.' Therefore, Michael probably remained more aware of his son's daily progress, and when he sensed some of the undesirable effects of the kind of environment he'd avoided when his mom originally fled the West Coast touching his son's life, he found additional impetus to do the same.

The New York move turned out to be a good one for all three Douglases. Although they retain residences in Santa Barbara and Los Angeles, New York has been their main base since 1984. Michael discovered that his reputation allowed him the freedom to continue working unhindered, and Diandra developed an interest in several philanthropic causes, including aid for the homeless, a very visible problem in the city. She convinced the Red Cross to collaborate and together they pulled off quite a coup – a premiere of *The Jewel of the Nile*, including a dinner and a raffle (with contributions by Kathleen Turner and Danny DeVito included) which raised $200,000 for the cause. She also became involved in major fund-raising for the Metropolitan Museum. 'It was certainly a shock to me, her organisational abilities,' Michael said. He wasn't the only admirer who gained an appreciation for Diandra. Mrs Douglas suddenly became quite the socialite, though she stresses that her party/luncheon outings are only a fragment of her life.

This fragment is not always shared with Michael, partially

because of his intense professional demands, and 'a lot of the time he simply doesn't want to go,' Diandra shrugs. 'If he is not inclined, I don't see why he should. But then I will go. And usually I go alone. I've always been very independent.' Michael counters, 'I like getting out, but I'm fortunate enough that because of my work I also have a cop-out.'

Apparently, the Douglases' marriage is supported by a framework of compromise and the ability to sustain the relationship through periods of separation on whatever level is possible. It is a fragile system, however, and occasionally it cracks under the weight of differing lifestyles and extended time apart. It is no secret that the Douglases have been separated several times, and not just geographically. Supposedly, Kirk has intervened and assisted in reconciling the couple on at least two rather public splits, but rumours concerning the couple's marital status have been flying about for many years.

Naturally, the tabloids focus on the 'other woman' angle, naming Kathleen Turner and brewery heiress Sabrina Guinness among the alleged throngs. Michael alternately denies and evades, but there have been strong indications that the gossip is true to some extent, though a confirmation of an explicit nature hasn't evidenced itself. Other talk alludes to an 'open marriage,' with one faction claiming it her idea, another his. The gossip increased as Diandra took on a part-time modelling career and Michael's star rose higher and higher with *Fatal Attraction* and *Wall Street*. Back in 1986, Diandra spoke of the difficulties in a guarded, yet somewhat revelatory way. 'The bottom line is we like each other. I try to be supportive of his work, which is an enormous burden he carries. And he is supportive of me. And it's interesting, now he has to deal with my career pursuits.

'Perhaps it is just a defence mechanism I have developed for peace of mind, but I don't feel jealousy anymore. I guess my theory is this: If Michael decides he loves another woman, I'd accept that. I wouldn't want to be with someone who didn't want to be with me.' It would seem from the slant of these and other comments, and several corroborating factors on Michael's part, that while infidelity is quite possibly a contributing problem, the Douglases' real problems may lie in another area altogether. After all, a spouse can compete with a distracting influence made of flesh and blood, if he or she chooses, but matters of a professional persuasion are touchy territory. Considering Michael's intense interludes with various projects in the years preceding his marriage, it is easy to determine what the main competition might be.

Michael himself attests to this indirectly when he speaks of his career thus: 'My work is a labour of love. Maybe that's why each project takes so long to do. I stick with it from beginning to end.' In Michael's case, 'from beginning to end' is a considerable commitment. *Cuckoo's Nest*, *The China Syndrome*, *Romancing the Stone* and even *Fatal Attraction* – all took over four years to complete. Often, one project runs into another, with no clear delineation. The rewards are obvious, but so too are the pitfalls. And Michael's feelings about these long-winded deals are never so apparent as when he himself points the metaphorical finger at them as the real 'other woman' in his life. 'Finding a good script is like falling in love with a girl,' he said in 1984. 'You read a script like you see a girl. You flirt with her a little bit and then you're hooked. You can't get her out of your mind, and that's what happens with my projects. It takes so long to make a movie and you can't get a divorce from it so you've got to make sure it's the right one.'

If Diandra is the person who Michael says she is, level-headed, logical, and intelligent, it would follow that her denial of jealousy is a truthful one. The only thing Michael seems to have loved in excess to Diandra and Cameron is his work. He's the first to admit to this particular love affair. 'I love my work and I'm really fortunate. It's an adult sandbox. It's make-believe. It allows you to learn about mental hospitals or nuclear power plants or to travel all over the jungle and meet charming and attractive and sexy people. It's a wonderful circus life, and I couldn't conceive of doing anything else.'

Movie work also provides Michael with the kind of support system he favours. Besides the advantages of being in a position to keep Joel close at hand and engage the talents of close friends like Danny DeVito, Michael can now afford to hire his own commune. Movie crews, especially those on location, tend to be rather clannish. It would seem that Michael discovered this refuge during *Cuckoo's Nest*, and embraced it ever after.

There is a darker side to Michael's fixation with movie-making. He states, 'I'm a fairly vindictive guy and I think that this can be channelled positively.' This sentiment crops up repeatedly, and in spite of Michael's 'Nice Guy' reputation, it appears that some of his motivating force comes from a lurking demon within, probably an unresolved leftover from his flaming youth period.

It is also entirely possible to trace Michael's negative aggressions back to Kirk. If he is his father's son, and all indications point to a more then genealogical connection, he's the possessor of a mighty temper and an aggressive streak a mile wide. In an attempt to forge his own identity, Michael evidently made an intense effort to sublimate many of his father's traits. Whatever actions he may have taken to beat his less-than-genteel impulses into submission have only succeeded to a certain extent (albeit an impressive one). The raging and angry forces of Michael's personality must have presented themselves in some fashion to Oliver Stone, when the producer surprised people by casting Michael Douglas as the thoroughly villainous Gorden Gekko.

Michael, aged 4, and Joel, aged 1½, with Kirk and Diana shortly before their separation. (AP/Wide World Photos)

Michael, aged 14, and Joel, aged 12, join little brothers Eric and Peter in wishing Spartacus a happy Father's Day. (AP/Wide World Photos)

During the shooting of *Cast a Giant Shadow* the family takes time out to pose, gathered around Joel as Santa Claus. (AP/Wide World Photos)

Michael and Kirk on the set of *Hail Hero.* (AP/Wide World Photos)

Early days in California. (Neal Peters Collection)

Michael and Karl Malden on *The Streets of San Francisco.* (Phototeque)

Michael and Diandra Douglas in New York. (Star File)

Kathleen Turner and Michael fight the wicked and rake in the dollars in the hugely successful *Romancing the Stone* (1984). (Phototeque)

Danny DeVito and Michael make funny faces and influence people at the opening party for *The Jewel of the Nile* in New York City. (Star File)

Michael and Kathleen Turner return as Jack and Joan in *The Jewel of the Nile* (1985). (Phototeque)

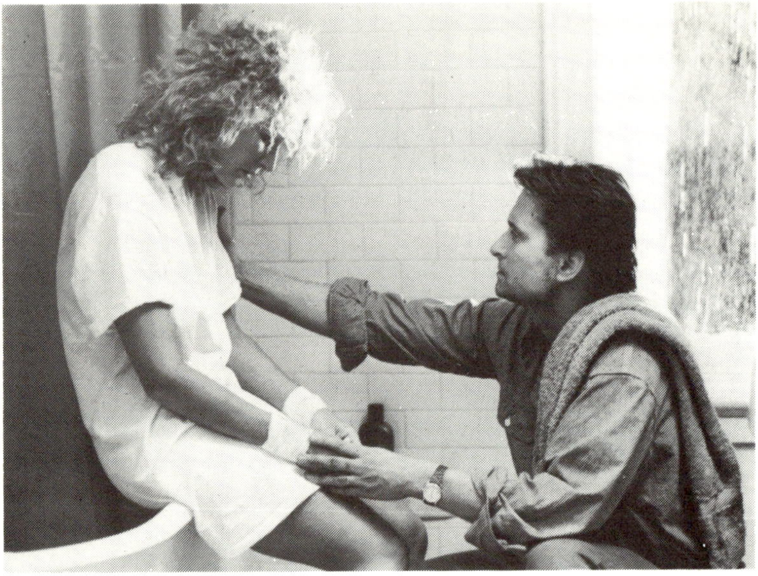

Michael as Dan comforts a distraught Glenn Close, Alex, in *Fatal Attraction*. (Phototeque)

Michael accepts his People's Choice Award for Best Actor in *Wall Street,* 1988. (AP/Wide World Photos)

Charlie Sheen and Michael as battling alter-egos in *Wall Street.* (Phototeque)

Wall Street's locker room confrontation. (Phototeque)

Michael, with presenter Marlee Matlin, and the ultimate prize, an Oscar for Best Actor, won for his portrayal of Gordon Gekko in *Wall Street.* (Star File)

Michael defines his entanglement with the business before he and Diandra married as exclusive. When Cameron was born, Michael made room for him as well. However, one can see the extent of his commitment: From the warm-up exercise of a role in *Coma* (his first post-marital project to appear) through his Oscar-winning performance in *Wall Street*, Michael Douglas remains a driven man.

Chapter Six

VARIOUS SYNDROMES

'There's not a lot of good material out there. I had to assume the responsibility of developing my own.'

– Michael Douglas, '84

'My biggest accomplishment was just sort of gaining the confidence to begin enjoying what I was doing. Acting for a long time was a struggle. I was the kind of guy who had the wastebasket right off stage in play productions and was puking my brains out. I was basically nervous and insecure and struggling with stage fright and even with film fright. I envied people who loved the camera. The camera to me always looked like my dentist's X-ray machine.'

– Michael Douglas, '84

The local news occasionally carries items guaranteed to agitate its viewers more than Third-World famine or war. Think of the rash of nursing home scandals in the New York area in the early Seventies, or those rare but disturbing cases of a nurse who hits the headlines by murdering patients rather than saving them. The horror of the situation is almost incomprehensible. We are conditioned to trust doctors from the first day a paediatrician waves a lollipop in our faces. However, there are incompetent or crazy doctors and nurses in the world, and bad hospitals do exist.

Dr Robin Cook tells a true story of a Boston hospital which continued implementing a certain procedure in spite of the fact that it killed approximately nine out of every ten people who submitted to it. The comparable mortality rate at a neighbouring hospital was 0.3. Dr Cook is famous for telling such stories, both actual and fictional, for he is the author of a string of best sellers blending hospitals and horror, exploiting our fear of scalpels that go clink in the night.

The ophthalmological surgeon turned novelist clinically constructed his first major novel, *Coma*, in the grand tradition of Dr Frankenstein – whom he credits as the original manifestation of medical phobia. First, he examined two hundred mysteries and their particular methods of creating fear and apprehension. 'It was a new challenge, like wiring my house,' the good doctor explained. 'I dissected why the reader's pulse increases and how the author gives and withholds information.' The results put *Coma* on the best seller list for six months, and a genre was reborn.

Best sellers of this stature are destined for the screen in some form. In this case, *Coma* made the journey from page to soundstage under the guiding hand of another doctor turned novelist, Michael Crichton. Dr Crichton wrote the screenplay (with some assistance from Dr Cook), directed the picture, and oversaw every detail of the production with Martin Ehrlichman. Together, they managed to construct a taut, suspenseful thriller, capturing the basic appeal of the novel and circumventing its more troublesome aspects without destroying its subtle overtones. Opportunities for sensationalising the story by dallying with its unlimited possibilities for gore-slinging were virtually ignored.

Besides its antiseptic setting, the movie featured another deviation from the norm: The protagonist is an independent, *female* doctor. Back in the 'dark ages' of the late Seventies, movies with four-million-dollar budgets rarely relied on a woman to carry them, unless that woman's name was Barbra Streisand. The preferred course of action was to perform a sex-change on the character; a little quick and painless surgery ensured the audience's easy acceptance.

Those involved in bringing *Coma* to the screen decided not to take the simple route, and relied on a strong story and good casting to win the public over. To strengthen the character of Susan Wheeler, they promoted her from intern (her title in the book) to surgeon. For the part they chose Genevieve Bujold, a young, talented, and, until recently, vastly underrated actress with an impressive list of credits.

Faced with the problem of casting an actor to play Dr Wheeler's fellow doctor, love interest, and second banana, Mark Bellows, Crichton and company selected Michael Douglas. Michael hadn't graced the screen, as they say, since his inauspicious efforts on behalf of Walt Disney in *Napoleon and Samantha* in 1972. Referring disparagingly to his past roles as 'my brief, gaudy hour in movies,' he assessed his pre-*Coma* film career as consisting of 'pictures with bad scripts, bad directors or both. This is the first time I've been offered a project with a good story laid out well, a good cast, and a good director.'

Those in charge agreed on Michael's suitability for the part 'because he and Bujold will look good together and because Michael has both the slightly pedantic quality necessary to make an audience believe he is a doctor and, in a script full of red herrings, enough ambiguity to leave you uncertain whose side he's on.' Michael also possessed the ability to stand back and allow Ms Bujold to inject Dr Wheeler with every ounce of fortitude required, without giving into any 'male'-ish inclinations to grab centre stage, or overcompensate for his relatively inactive role. In fact, Mr Douglas is so laid back that occasionally his own tie overpowers him.

Bellows is portrayed as a professionally conservative doctor on his way up the ladder; half willing to engage in hospital politics, and half resentful of their childish idiosyncrasies. He vacillates between pride for assertive professional equal Dr Wheeler and a kind of uneasy aggravation at her refusal to slip into a traditional woman's role in their relationship. This emotional fence-straddling is established in a neat, virtually uninterrupted monologue which Douglas delivers during his first significant appearance in the movie. His casual and effortless manner holds no evidence of the thirty-five takes preceding this fine execution, but for Michael those thirty-five takes were perhaps the most gruesome aspect of the film.

In brief, *Coma* details Dr Wheeler's determined mission to prove that something is amiss in the hospital when her friend succumbs to an inexplicable coma after a simple operation. She proceeds rapidly through a dizzying series of incidents which lead her to the Jefferson Institute, a clearing house for black market organs masquerading as a low-cost, highly efficient haven for the brain dead. A misunderstanding, and her justifiably mounting paranoia, alienates her from Mark and leads her to rely on the fatherly chief of surgery (competently portrayed by Richard Widmark), who, unbeknownst to her, stands to lose the most if her discoveries are revealed.

There are many elements at work in back and foreground. Especially notable are those picked from the pocket of 'the master of suspense.' According to *Los Angeles Times* critic Charles Champlin, '*Coma* aspires to the Hitchcock genre in which the chills and the laughs stay close together in the dark, and the frights are reassuringly make-believe and funny. . . .

Where *Coma* follows Hitchcock very well indeed is in its creation of an innocent caught up in events she does not understand and whose cries of alarm, once she does see the lurking evil, no one will believe. Like the best detective stories, *Coma* serves up as many red herrings as a Scandinavian restaurant. . . . There's little enough support at Bujold's home hospital; even her fellow surgical resident, Michael Douglas, thinks it's all in her mind. He's ambitious to be head resident and she's a threat to his image. The ambiguity about Douglas – nice guy or bad guy – is cleverly set up and well played.'

Michael's finest moment in the film comes at the end when Dr Wheeler is felled after many attempts by a 'Mickey' in her Scotch administered by the chief. Through speedy deduction, Bellows realises that Susan's incumbent and sudden operation will prove fatal to her. He submerges his previous inclination to write off her actions as those of a hysterical female, and, most importantly, admits to himself that he was wrong.

Much of Dr Bellows's inner turbulence is communicated by Douglas's facial expressions and body language, in a form reminiscent of some of his finer moments on 'The Streets of San Francisco', and a tribute to the skills he developed there. After the harrowing rescue, there is no defensiveness or condescension in his attitude toward the still-prone Dr Wheeler. Instead, he is a picture of quiet outrage, directed exclusively at the man whose greed has tainted and trod upon everything he held estimable about his profession.

In a sense, it is the character of Mark Bellows that gains a new maturity in the movie, in contrast to the novel's inclusion of this complexity as an aspect of Dr Wheeler's character. This clever switch adds depth to Michael Douglas's performance and creates an interesting subtext. It's not surprising that he would be called on in the future to portray a long line of 'sensitive guys'.

Prior to 1979, public knowledge of the prevalent dangers inherent in utilising nuclear energy remained anchored in the Stone Age. Antinuke activism barely constituted a fringe phenomenon, the fanatical pursuit of egg-headed environmentalists, never-say-die hippie radicals, and assorted sprout-chompers. In those pre-Chernobyl days, nuclear disasters still inhabited the realm of science fiction.

The public experienced a rude awakening on March 28, 1978, when the Three Mile Island power plant began percolating. By coincidence, *The China Syndrome*, Michael Douglas's first production since *One Flew Over the Cuckoo's Nest*, had opened nationwide in over 650 theatres just twelve days earlier.

Until then, the topic of potential radioactive leakage was considered documentary fodder. The difficulty of translating the convoluted technical and political abstractions involved into common parlance kept commercial filmmakers at bay; exploring the issue in an informative, relevant *and* entertaining manner seemed beyond the scope of both major and underground companies.

Tom S. Cook and Michael Gray's script for what eventually became *The China Syndrome** came into Michael Douglas's possession shortly after *Cuckoo's Nest* made its grand showing at the Oscars. Hoping to reestablish himself as a presence on the big screen, Michael sought a special property – a good vehicle for him to co-star in.

The finished screenplay version of *The China Syndrome* introduces us to Kimberly Wells (played by Jane Fonda), a prim, pretty newscaster employed at TV station KXLA. She and Richard Adams (Michael Douglas), her mini-cam toting sidekick, are shooting a short documentary on energy at a local

*The project's name changed from *Eyewitness to Power* before finally settling on the release title.

nuclear power plant when an 'accident' occurs, nearly causing the reactor to blow its top.

Plant supervisor Jack Godell (Jack Lemmon) narrowly averts disaster, but certain curious side effects of the near catastrophe have left him with residual doubts about the plant's safety. Probing deeper, he discovers that a contractor has deliberately falsified documents pertaining to key pipe weldings in the reactor's fail-safe system. Excessive strain such as might occur during an emergency, or even full power operation, could break the pipes and cause the phenomenon the film takes its title from: the China Syndrome.

More commonly referred to as a nuclear 'meltdown', the reactor core gets so hot that the bottom drops out and begins boring its way through the earth. Theoretically, it could sink to the other side of the globe (hence China), but, more likely, the heat source would hit a water table and burst into a cloud of radioactive steam. The cloud would then rise and spread by wind currents, potentially contaminating vast areas.

Wells and Adams convince Godell to publicise the revealing documents to prevent construction of another plant and defuse the disaster brewing at the existing one. But a courier bearing the sensitive documents gets assassinated, the documents are stolen, and Godell is chased to the gates of the plant by the murderers.

Once inside the plant, Godell takes over the control room at gunpoint and holds the reactor 'hostage'. Unless he gets the TV coverage he demands, the plant, he threatens, will be blown skyhigh. Wells and Adams arrange his telecast, but before Godell can expose the corrupt power company and its dangerous reactor, a SWAT team bursts in and shoots him dead.

As Godell had predicted, a meltdown nearly transpires; however in the subsequent cover-up, Godell is discredited as a violent loony. In the end, Kimberly Wells stands up to the power company and challenges the cover-up on TV, leaving us with the hope that the truth will out, Godell will be vindicated, and the pronuke baddies vanquished.

The story's duality excited Michael. Its deadly serious anti-nuclear statement came equipped with a commercially viable suspense-thriller element. *The China Syndrome* attracted him on a thematic level as well. 'I found this parallel with *Cuckoo's Nest*,' Michael explained. 'Individuals caught in a corporate or social structure that forces them to make a moral decision at the sacrifice of losing their lives. It's an effort at what is basically Greek tragedy.'

Fortified by the weight of the Oscar in his pocket, Michael overestimated the influence he could wield over the Hollywood community. He couldn't predict the interpersonal problems that would delay the production for four years.

Problem number one concerned Mike Gray, who wanted to sit in the director's chair. Michael supported this notion, but unfortunately Gray's only previous filmmaking experiences were derived from low-budget documentaries. Allowing a novice to direct a controversial film spelled potential disaster as far as the major studios were concerned. With Gray at the helm, the safest course was a strong cast with built-in box office appeal . . . if those big names would agree to settle for a bit less than their accustomed fee.

Twice-blessed Oscar winner Jack Lemmon considered the wage cut worthwhile; he'd been waiting for a project like *The China Syndrome* for two decades. The subject matter jibed with his personal and professional interest in environmental causes: In the early Seventies, Mr Lemmon narrated a series of documentaries for NBC pertaining to ecological problems. Protestations from the Pacific Gas and Electric Company effected the cancellation of one particularly scathing episode dealing with the negative facets of nuclear energy.

When *The China Syndrome* appeared, Lemmon snapped up the role of Jack Godell. 'I stayed out of work a year to do this little mother,' he said. 'I'm proud as hell to be in the damn film.' Lemmon was equally enthusiastic about his producer: 'What I love about Michael is he finally got *Cuckoo* off the ground and made one of the great, great films. He's bright, he's talented, but mainly he cares. That son of a bitch came up to my house and he was *passionate*. This was the film he wanted to do.'

Not all the original candidates for the cast were as selflessly enthusiastic as Mr Lemmon. Initially, Jack Nicholson considered taking one of the lead roles, but this plan quickly fell through for unrevealed reasons. While Douglas attempted to attract Columbia Pictures' interest, he cast himself as the film crew producer and Richard Dreyfuss as the crew's main figure. However, Dreyfuss priced himself right out of the picture by suddenly doubling his fee to $500,000.* Michael found himself in an uncomfortable position: 'I was left with my thumb up my ass.'

Robert Redford was approached as a possible replacement for Dreyfuss. Mr Redford found the script viable, but he passed. 'As an actor I am looking for something different than the character in *The China Syndrome*,' he stated in a letter to Michael.

Meanwhile, Jane Fonda's IPC company and Columbia were working on a deal to produce a film with an antinuclear slant. Originally, Fonda was interested in portraying Karen Silkwood,** but 'there were a half dozen people trying to do the

*Dreyfuss attributed this somewhat foolhardy move to his 'reservations' about Gray's directorial abilities, but it may be that certain personal problems Dreyfuss was experiencing at the time contributed to his desire for large amounts of cash.

**This was prior to Meryl Streep's *Silkwood*.

Karen Silkwood story at the same time,' according to Bruce Gilbert, Fonda's business partner in IPC. Ultimately, Fonda lost the battle over the story rights and decided to join forces with Douglas's team on *The China Syndrome*. 'Michael came along with the script, which I read and immediately felt was real exciting,' Ms Fonda elucidated.

Fonda's participation in the project invited speculation that elements of the Silkwood yarn would be assimilated into the film. A scene written into the film confirmed this: When Richard Adams's assistant is forced off the road and incriminating documents are stolen by pronuke bad guys, it strongly echoed the suspicious circumstances surrounding Silkwood's death.

Fonda's demands soon overwhelmed Mike Gray's visions: where Gray wanted an 'untraditional' look for the film, Fonda insisted on a straightforward Hollywood treatment more palatable to mass taste. Gray observed, 'Suddenly the budget jumps $2 billion and they say, "Okay, who's this guy here in the corner?" ' Gradually pressured out of the director's seat, Mike Gray resented Fonda's influence. 'Although Jane Fonda is politically radical,' complained Gray, 'professionally she is quite conservative.'

James Bridges (Oscar nominee for *The Paper Chase*) replaced Gray. Starting as a TV and film actor, Bridges scripted such classics as *Colossus: The Forbin Project*, before scoring his first directorial gig, *The Baby Maker* (a surrogate motherhood melodrama). His post-*China Syndrome* accomplishments include the ever-popular *Urban Cowboy*, the utterly reviled *Mike's Murder, Perfect*, and *Bright Lights, Big City*.

By means of deftly executed sex change, Bridges installed Jane Fonda as *China Syndrome's* lead character. Fonda, inspired by a *Los Angeles Times* series on media consultants, fleshed out Kimberly Wells by making her a 'happy-news' reporter aspiring to the investigative big leagues. Diandra Douglas (under the pseudonym Diandra Morrell) squeezed into the film as a newscaster ready to fill Fonda's shoes when she's late for a broadcast. Some party scenes including Diandra (which she appeared in for 'fun') were cut from the final print.

Although Michael Gray believed that Douglas modelled Richard Adams, the 'loud-mouthed punk documentary filmmaker,' after himself, Michael actually accompanied professional TV newscameramen on their rounds to study their work habits. (One of the cameramen he tagged along with was Bob Brown, the NBC cameraman who later died at the Jonestown massacre in Guyana.) For expert information in the field of atomic energy, Michael employed a team of technical advisers. The team included three former General Electric consultants who resigned from the company due to its policies on nuclear safety.

James Bridges described Michael Douglas as 'meticulous, dogged, totally creative . . . But most of all he's a lot of fun.' But Bridges never confused Michael the actor with Mr Douglas the producer. 'Doing one particular sequence,' recalled Bridges, 'Michael as producer kept nagging me, "Hurry up we're days behind . . . we've got to get out of here." I left, until the last shot, a close-up of him as star. "Take one, action . . . cut, print." One take. Of course I knew the take was just fine, though ultimately we didn't end up using it in the final cut.'

The chance synchronisation of the film's release and the Three Mile Island incident gave a stamp of credibility to a story which otherwise might have been dismissed as a liberal paranoid fantasy. Whether the film would have provoked equivalent impact without the 'front page' support will never be known, but for Michael the lucky coincidence was 'a religious experience'.

According to a Columbia spokesman, business for *China*

Syndrome was respectable well before the accident, but unexpected publicity generated by the near holocaust was a decided boon. Just three weeks after release, it accrued almost $20 million in US receipts.

From Columbia's point of view, public alarm over Three Mile Island guaranteed a sense of immediacy about the film's topic which spelled audience staying power. But in retrospect, Douglas believes differently: 'Contrary to what people thought, Three Mile Island was not an asset but a detriment. What we had portrayed as an edge-of-your-seat thriller became *real*. People started thinking that they saw our movie on the CBS Evening News. They avoided it because it was too real.'

Around Harrisburg, Pennsylvania, where the accident occurred, the thin line between reality and fantasy stretched to near breaking. Moviegoers emerging from local theatres after viewing *China Syndrome* were greeted by battalions of reporters who besieged them with questions about their hometown . . . questions not dissimilar to the ones Fonda and Douglas raised on screen.

Columbia's official policy was to downplay any connection between the movie and Three Mile Island and the studio placed a general clamp on all press and TV appearances. Even before the movie came out, Douglas stayed tight-lipped about its subject: 'I know this is a really good picture, but somehow I can't shake the feeling that if you tell someone upfront too many times how terrific something is they tend to have a letdown when they see it.'

At no time did Columbia directly refer to the real-life events amplifying *China Syndrome*'s drama. Columbia's initial 'teaser' ads for the film prophetically read, 'Only a handful of people know what *The China Syndrome* means. Soon you will know.' In the event of the film's success, Columbia prepared a follow-up ad reading, 'The most controversial film of our time. Over 10 million people know what *The China Syndrome* means. Do you?' Jack Brodsky, Columbia VP in charge of advertising* claimed the ad campaign remained unchanged from their original designs prepared months in advance. 'We bent over backwards to dissociate ourselves from the situation,' said Brodsky. 'It's far too serious an issue to exploit.'

Perhaps behind closed doors theatre owners were greedily rubbing their hands, but upfront they paid lip service to the serious nature of the situation. 'It's too drastic even to think of promoting business on the basis of this,' admonished Spike Tadaroff, manager of a Harrisburg theatre that showed *China Syndrome*. 'I must admit, though, it's a godsend that this movie is playing at the time this happened. It's going to help business. It is helping business.'

Michael Douglas postponed an appearance on 'The Tonight Show' until the crisis abated. Lemmon also cooperated with the publicity blackout, and cancelled an appearance on a CBS special about Three Mile Island. Jane Fonda chose to speak out but emphasised in her press conference that she opined solely as an individual, not a representative of the film.

Editorial preoccupation with *China Syndrome*'s message and its relation to recent events left the cinematic virtues or vices of the movie somewhat underexamined. Generally it engendered admiration as a well-crafted suspense, which still holds true, although the protagonists seem laughably urgent at times.

As a loud-mouthed, hot-tempered hippie, Michael is quite believable, and his reading of Richard Adams is consistent with the screen persona he brought to fruition in later films: a kind, sincere mensch disguised as an Oscar Madisonesque cynic. Fonda has the movie's lead part, but Kimberly Wells operates

*Brodsky later became a bigwig at Michael Douglas's Bigstick Productions.

primarily as a static observer, reacting to the events unfolding around her.

Richard Adams, on the other hand, like Godell, motivates the dramatic impetus of the story. Adams is a mover: his decisive actions, founded on a conspicuous sense of integrity, set events in motion and he has the gumption to back up his beliefs. Whether sneaking a shot of the reactor's top-secret nerve centre or condemning his superiors as 'chicken shit', Adams is a man to keep your eyes on and Douglas played him with zealous fervour.

This same fiery conviction inhabited the soul of Michael's next screen role, Michael Adropolis, the marathon competitor in *Running*, but this character's burning ideals were expressed in an altogether different mode of behaviour. Competitiveness and self-discipline are Andropolis's tools for making something of a life marred by failure.

Andropolis's main problem is that he can't finish anything he begins. A thirty-year-old loser, he suffers from a ruined marriage (his wife leaves him for a car dealer), a miserable job as a stock boy (he gets canned), and a terrible collegiate track record (he's a 'choke artist'). In other words, when the going gets tough, Andropolis drops out.

From the depths of rock-bottom self-esteem, Michael Andropolis picks himself up by his bootstraps and enters the Olympic marathon. Predictably enough, he overcomes extraordinary odds and finishes the race, thus fulfilling the movie's worthy but sentimentally ensconced little-engine-that-could 'message.'

Completed a year before *The China Syndrome*, *Running*, though released in its aftermath, benefitted only meagrely from the crest of acclaim Michael was riding. It is notable, if for nothing else, as his first true starring role since *Hail, Hero!* Michael judged *Running* the best script submitted to him at the time. 'I cried when I read it. I must have read hundreds of screenplays looking for something like this.' It's apparent how a story which brings some of the aspects of the Douglas/Danielovitch mythology into a more contemporary mode would affect Michael so deeply.

Just before his initial flirtation with production, Michael began finding pleasure purely in the craft of acting. 'After I got out of the TV series and produced *Cuckoo's Nest*,' he explained, 'there was this false image that I wasn't interested in acting any more; but I was. The problem was to find a screenplay that really touched me in some way – dramatically, comically. . . . I did *Coma* because it scared me; *Running* moved me.'

Suspecting he wasn't judging the script objectively enough, Michael had family members look it over for approval. 'It has to do with my being a romantic,' he said. 'I'm a soft touch for emotion, which is the antithesis to the hard-ass character of American films.

'Everyone goes to the movies hoping to be moved one way or the other, which is part of the magic of making movies. *Running* is a wonderful love story and sport. I liked aspects in the script of the family trying to get back together. We all have periods in our lives where we feel we are losers.'

Although not a runner at the time he read the script, Michael underwent rigorous physical conditioning to achieve the physique of a world-class marathoner. 'I had to get in shape for it and it wasn't easy,' he affirmed. 'At first I couldn't run around the block without getting the dry heaves. I was appalled at the condition I was in – particularly since my father is in such good shape. I kept going and pretty soon I'd worked my way up to sixteen miles at a time. My weight dropped by fifteen pounds. I stopped smoking and I began to feel terrific.' By the end, Michael was logging an impressive sixty miles per week through daily 6:30 a.m. workouts. 'I haven't been in such good shape since school,' he proudly acknowledged.

Douglas devoured books and magazines on running and analysed the sport on film. In his early training he eschewed the use of a stopwatch, but would work with competitive runners in order to check his form. By the time principal photography for *Running* began, Michael could run a seven-minute marathon mile.

Running's director Steven Stern scoffed at Michael, 'You're mad . . . the most you'll have to run for the camera is half a mile,' but Michael persisted in his training and his beefy transformation is evidenced on film. 'Although the director laughed at me,' Michael recounted, 'that training period paid off. There's a look to professional runners and you can't fake it.' Intercutting with ABC-TV stock footage from the 1976 Montreal Olympics, Michael boasted, 'What we've got looks really good.'

Apart from a minor toe ailment common among joggers, Michael derived many personal benefits from his self-imposed regimen: 'Since I began running, I sleep better, have a better disposition and more energy . . . more endurance energy versus nervous energy, more stamina. I'm in finer physical shape and my mind is sharper.' He also testified that running was 'fabulous for hangovers'.

Running was financed for about $3,500,000 by both American and Canadian sources, including the Canadian Film Development Corporation, a Canadian federal agency that alone invested half a million. The combined possibilities of publicising *Running* in conjunction with both the upcoming Olympic games and the then-flourishing jogging craze, indicated strong sales potential for the movie. Before completion, *Running* was pre-sold both to ABC, who agreed not to broadcast it until two years after theatrical release and Viacom, who purchased the syndication rights.

'The presence of a TV star in a movie can help the sale of

a movie to television,' executive producer Douglas explained. 'When you're in a series that is watched by thirty million people once a week, the impact is unbelievable. My father has been a movie star for years, and when we'd go out together someplace, he was amazed at the attention *I'd* get because of the series.

'Now an actor's career is more like a professional athlete's; you don't have a steady development, you go in waves. . . . The only way to be an actor is to be successful; you're not acting if nobody's watching.'

Critics did watch, but they didn't like what they saw. Andropolis, as a character, aroused little sympathy; Gene Siskel, for example, described Andropolis as a 'sanctimonious heel' and denounced *Running* as 'easily one of the year's worst movies.' Michael Douglas, for all his effusiveness about the role, had hitched his star to a turkey.

It's My Turn, Michael's subsequent venture, fared mildly better at the hands of the critics, but, relegated to a supporting role, Michael was received merely as a component of the cast and not cited for any singular praise. He portrays a young baseball player, prematurely retired due to injury, embroiled in a tense, amorous affair with Jill Clayburgh, gifted mathematician and his newly met stepsister.

A low-key, episodically constructed film, *It's My Turn*'s main thrust was contemplation of the intricacies of 'relationships,' particularly those of young professionals, and the external forces that prevail upon them. Neither a feminist tract, nor strictly a 'woman's film' (though both written and directed by women), *It's My Turn* examined intelligently, if somewhat inconclusively, the complications that arise when careers, parents, and ambitions co-mingle with basic boy-girl interaction.

It's My Turn was directed by Claudia Weill, whose previous film, *Girlfriends*, delved into many of the same issues. For Michael, being directed by a female was a joy: 'I have not had many directors come up to me and say, "You are such a dish." I am spoiled.' He also inferred that he was a bit envious of the attention female stars attract from male directors. 'There is a moment every actor has,' Michael observed, 'when the director goes over to the leading lady, puts his arms around her shoulders, walks her around, and whispers, "What's wrong, darling? Let's talk." And you stand there like a bump on a log. Well, I'm sorry, guys like to be complimented too. I just loved having the director come up to me, put her arm around my shoulders and ask if I'm okay. She made me feel confident.'

Michael held Claudia Weill in the highest regard, so he was somewhat dismayed when, after its release, a gossip column item appeared stating that Michael despised *It's My Turn* and refused to promote it. 'I never said that,' Michael protested. 'What I said was that I couldn't shoot my wad like I did with *The China Syndrome*. I am overexposed. I told them I was willing to do some interviews, but not to count on me for all the talk shows. I am an actor, and I cannot go out like that after every film. That's what I said.'

Apparently the source of the rumour was the office of producer Ray Stark, who'd brought the film to Columbia Pictures in the first place. Douglas, who had his own separate production deal with Columbia, found the situation embarrassing and precarious and felt compelled to formally explain that he hadn't gone around bad-mouthing Columbia's movie. 'The whole thing was planted,' Michael concluded. 'It was some kind of manipulative thing. . . . I decided the best thing was to let it pass. I called Claudia, who was shocked, and explained that I had never said it.'

Worn out by the sustained efforts of his past three movies, Michael took an extended break from acting after *It's My Turn*. 'My obligation is to myself and my family,' he told *Variety*, and for the next few years, Michael devoted himself to shooting baby pictures instead of movies.

Granddaddy Kirk frequently visited the Douglas household to fawn over his first grandson. Michael would jestingly complain that Polaroids of his son were usually obliterated by close-ups of Kirk's ubiquitous jaw, with Cameron reduced to a little out-of-focus baby bundle in the corner.

Proud papa Michael made a modest assessment of his cinematic accomplishments when in a 1979 interview with *Women's Wear Daily*, he implored the readership to 'Think of me as an actor . . . or at least as a daddy.'

Chapter Seven

ROMANCING

'I never really feel successful. There are always things you'd like to change. But I think I'm beginning to accept the imperfections. It's a big step. I know it sounds perfect but it hasn't really been easy. Understand I'm not complaining. I'm very happy, but it has been a lot of work.'

– Michael Douglas, '84

'Just because you've had a couple of successes doesn't mean the studios automatically say yes to you . . .'

– Michael Douglas (*Los Angeles Times*, 5/13/84)

The late 1970s saw two huge financial successes for Michael Douglas – *One Flew Over the Cuckoo's Nest* and *The China Syndrome* – and a couple of feebler efforts destined to remain forgettable. After pocketing a respectable sum for his efforts, Michael apparently grew tired of rushing around, scraping together independent backing for his ventures.

In 1979, upon returning from a brief Parisian vacation with his wife and son, Michael plunged into a new business deal that he hoped would allow him to devote more time to the artistic side of motion pictures. He signed a three-year contract with Columbia Pictures wherein they agreed to finance his semi-independent production company, Bigstick, covering all overhead and staff salaries, and compensating Douglas for any movies he made. Jack Brodsky, a Hollywood veteran (producer of *Little Murders* and Woody Allen's *Everything You Always Wanted to Know About Sex*) and former advertising/publicity VP for Columbia, joined Bigstick as executive vice-president.

Columbia Pictures chief Leo Jaffe boasted that the deal with Douglas was 'a coup for him and for us,' adding, 'We're looking for pictures we can mutually agree upon.' Under Columbia's auspices, Douglas believed he could produce 'a picture a year.' As it turned out, Bigstick Productions made nothing for the next four years.

Ironically, the very first project that Douglas selected for Columbia (and his first abortive effort) eventually evolved into a highly successful movie. Michael purchased the rights to a book entitled *Virgin Kisses* by Gloria Nagy – a suspense yarn dealing with lust destroying a married man's life. Eight years and numerous rewrites later, this basic premise mutated into *Fatal Attraction.*

The most promising of the projects Bigstick initiated in 1980 was a script created by Bruce A. Evans and Raynold Gideon, *Starman.* But by its 1984 release, its earlier promise was long belied: *Starman* was better known through the movie industry as the film Columbia decided to make *instead* of Steven Spielberg's *ET The Extraterrestrial.*

Both *ET* and *Starman* were under development at Columbia during 1980, and both shared similar plots – a stranded alien befriends a lonely earthling who assists him in evading pursuers. But unlike *ET, Starman* took a slightly more adult stance.

Jeff Bridges plays the awkward but engaging 'starman,' accidentally Earthbound during an observational visit. Karen Allen is his reluctant chauffeur in a cross-country race against the clock for Bridge's rendezvous with his mother ship. Complications arise from Bridge's precise physical duplication of Allen's deceased husband, and her growing feelings for him/it.

According to one studio source, 'Columbia passed on *ET* because they were going to make *Starman*.' Frank Price, head of Columbia during part of Bigstick's residency there, eventually allowed Spielberg to make *ET* first, confident in *Starman*'s ability to transcend the competition. 'We always perceived it as a wonderful love story that just happened to be set against a science-fiction background,' explained supervising executive Robert Lawrence. However, while *ET* was completed and released, *Starman*'s woes only multiplied and it fell increasingly behind schedule.

While Douglas wasn't particularly interested in sci-fi, he loved 'the wonderful idea of this woman showing the alien the absurdities of our planet and not meaning to do so. Everything in the world made sense to [the alien] except human behaviour. I liked the concept.'

Douglas liked the concept so much he considered taking the role for himself at one point, even though he announced, 'We're looking for an unknown first. That's not the easiest thing to find.' Apparently it was *too* difficult for some people to deal with: shooting slated to commence in the fall of '82 with director John Badham was cancelled when Badham backed out, and rewrites were ordered. By spring of the following year, the project still floated in limbo, lacking both director and cast.

ET's mammoth success made the unenviable job of writer Dean Reisner (called in for rewrites after the original script-writers' second draft was rejected) even harder. For more than two years Reisner laboured over *Starman*, emphasising the love-story angle of the plot, while diminishing aspects of the story that bore an uncomfortable resemblance to *ET*.

Meanwhile, a rhumba line of directors paraded through the unlucky project, including Adrian Lyne, Michael Mann, and Tony Scott. Finally, John Carpenter (*Halloween, The Fog, The Thing*) took over, but Columbia continued to hedge about a definite release date. 'We had *Tootsie* in development for four years,' explained former Columbia chief Frank Price. 'If you're trying to make exceptional pictures (which is what Michael, all of us, are trying to do), it takes time.'

Michael Douglas, however, ascribed Columbia's procrastination to a more commercial motivation: 'What's happened to the movie business is market research. You would think, and I *did* think that "Here I am, I've produced two big movies," and I go to the studio with a new thing I want to do. I've got a track record, but it turns out that doesn't matter.' Whatever the real reasons for the delay, *Starman* didn't appear until 1984.

In the film's credits John Carpenter included a dedication to Dean Reisner, author of *Starman*'s last five drafts. Despite his significant contributions, Reisner's billing as a co-screenwriter was denied by a Writer's Guild arbitration awarding exclusive credit to its original authors, Evans and Gideon. Considering Carpenter's dedication a violation of their ruling, the Guild threatened to force Columbia to destroy all copies of the film that bore the embattled credit. Matters were complicated even further when a novelisation of the story came out with front cover credits for Evans, Gideon, *and* Reisner.

Distracted by other projects, Douglas gradually phased himself out of the production's ups and downs. While satisfied with *Starman*'s outcome, Michael barely contributed to the final result, apart from some casting decisions and making notes on an early cut.

Starman garnered mostly favourable reviews (critics praised it as a visually elegant 'genteel fantasy'), but it was no blockbuster. Its final gasp came two years later with the premiere of ABC's short-lived prime time series loosely based on the same story. Starring Robert Hays as the alien, the show endured for a couple of seasons before floating off into the stratosphere.

Michael's acting career around this time wasn't exactly going like gangbusters either. His role as a young, idealistic judge in 20th Century-Fox's 1983 release *The Star Chamber* was his first time before the lenses since *It's My Turn* in 1980. He attributed his prolonged absence from the silver screen to two excuses: 'I wanted to spend time with my wife and son . . . I had a skiing accident that led to a blood virus ailment and I was laid up for a long time.'

The Star Chamber was a respectable if inconspicuous screen comeback for Michael. In a summer movie season dominated by sci-fi movies and teensploitation flicks (*War Games*, a big 1983 summer hit managed to combine both genres), *The Star Chamber* stood out from the rest of the pack with its dark musings on the ambiguities of the judicial system.

The screenplay, co-written by Roderick Taylor and director Peter Hyams (also responsible for *Outland* and *Capricorn One*) concerns a judge (Michael Douglas) forced by legal technicalities to free murder suspects he's convinced are truly guilty. The frustrated judge is initiated by his elder colleagues into a group known as The Group – a clandestine society that metes out vigilante justice unhindered by legal restraints.*

Michael Douglas joins The Group but when a suspect is unfairly convicted, Douglas decides to blow the whistle on the whole operation. Despite the efforts of an assassin hired by The Group to stop Douglas, justice prevails.

*'Star chamber proceedings' nowadays signify acts of an arbitrary tribunal.

Tom Sherak, then president of 20th Century-Fox's marketing and distribution, conceded that the company had bucked against the summer trend by releasing a heavyweight movie about legal issues during a season traditionally devoted to light entertainment. The rationale, he explained, was that the film would succeed by contrast: 'We think it's the perfect way to offset the summer. When we saw the summer schedule of releases, we could see it would be a summer for four-to-eight-year-olds and thought we could counter that programming.'

A high saturation TV campaign was launched with spots that misleadingly glorified the vigilante shenanigans the movie opposed. Despite Schwarzeneggerish promotions, the film failed to catch on – not least because of its title. 'There was a feeling it was a trouble title,' Sherak admitted. 'It sounded like another science-fiction film instead of what it is – a serious, well-made drama.'

Sherak's trepidation about the title was well warranted. *Variety* film reviewer Jim Harwood complained that the film makers displayed 'an excess of faith in today's filmgoing audience if they think the bulk of today's filmgoing audience will know the title's fifteenth-century derivation as an extra-judicial body (many are still struggling with the meaning of the first thirteen stars in the American flag).'

Competent performance by Douglas notwithstanding, the apathetic response of critics and audiences alike caused *The Star Chamber* to adjourn swiftly and unmourned. With two falling *Stars* on his hands, Michael looked to his third production for an upswing in his fortunes. That production was *Romancing the Stone*.

'One of the worst movie titles I've ever heard,' lamented *At the Movies* critic Gene Siskel. Judging from the bafflement elicited by the title, one would have thought that *Romancing the Stone* would suffer the same sort of public misapprehension that caused *Star Chamber* to fail; instead it emerged as one of Douglas's biggest triumphs.

Completed at a below average cost of $9.5 million, *Romancing the Stone* was, by *Variety*'s account, one of the top box office draws of 1984. It sold $20 million worth of tickets in its first two and a half weeks, and earned an additional $15 million within thirty days. By 1986, it had grossed over $100 million.

The film's origins were humble enough: Diane Renee Thomas, a thirty-three-year-old waitress (who worked at either the Corla Beach Cantina, a Pacific Coast Highway Mexican restaurant, or Alice's Restaurant in Malibu Beach, depending on which legend you subscribe to) composed the script in her spare time. She was still employed as a waitress when, a year later, Bigstick's Jack Brodsky stumbled across her screenplay. Brodsky thought the script had commercial potential and submitted it to his boss, Michael Douglas. Less than a week later, Douglas bought the story for $250,000.

Douglas found Thomas's neophyte, fresh, and unjaded approach to screenwriting attractive. 'It just had a spontaneity about the writing,' Michael enthused. 'She was not cautious. The script had a wonderful spirit about it. . . . There was a total lack of fear to the writing. It worked.' He marvelled at its 'wonderful, virginal quality. After *China Syndrome*, I'd o.d.'d on grimness.'

The tonic Diane devised was the tale of a shy, single romance novelist, Joan Wilder, whose sister Gloria is kidnapped by Colombian thugs. Gloria's late husband had mailed a treasure map to Joan in New York which Gloria tells Joan she must bring to Colombia in order to rescue her.

When Joan arrives in Colombia she undergoes a series of misadventures entirely foreign to the docile, protected lifestyle she's used to. Joan battles drug smugglers, soldiers, alligators, and a host of criminals, not the least a murderous paramilitary leader (posing as head of the Department of Antiquities) who also wants the treasure map.

Among these lowlifes, she also meets the man of her dreams, the ultimate lowlife – Jack T. Colton, vagabond adventurer in search of fortune.

Colton convinces Joan that the only way to save her sister is to fetch the treasure – a large valentine-shaped emerald known as '*El Corazón*.' At times Colton is shady and manipulative, but in the end he proves loyal, opting to save Joan rather than retrieve the jewel from a runaway crocodile's belly. When Jack dives into a croc-infested lake, Joan fears it's the last she'll ever see of him. But Colton reappears in New York with the sailboat of *his* dreams, and together they sail off down West End Avenue, to embark upon their round-the-world cruise.

When Bigstick first purchased the rights to this story back in '79, Michael hadn't intended to appear in the movie at all; the project interested him first and foremost as a producer. But several actors to whom he offered Colton's part refused it, including one Sylvester Stallone (who, after seeing the film, regretted passing it up). 'At the time the script was presented to me,' grunted Stallone, 'it wasn't ready. It was too literal, too basic; it wasn't fun. Back then, I didn't have the insight to imagine what it could be. I give Michael real credit.'

The main complaint of the actors was that the female lead was the key role. 'They were right of course,' Douglas admitted. 'It was then that I decided to play the role myself.' This decision notwithstanding, as late as 1982 Douglas still told the press that he planned to fill the cast exclusively with *non-major* names.

In a way, Jack Colton was just the role Michael needed. He yearned for a character with a bit of edge to it, to contrast with his bland counterparts in *Coma*, *Running*, and *It's My Turn*. 'It's boring to play good guys,' he explained, echoing Dad's sentiments from several decades earlier. 'It really is. You look at most stars that made it. . . . That one part where they play a bastard. . . . People find it very attractive – women are attracted to someone who's bad. It's a very interesting thing; they like a little nastiness.'

Michael intended to put *Romancing* into production for Columbia in 1980, but the project got so bogged down in script and casting problems that Columbia finally decided to pass. As soon as the three-year overhead deal between Bigstick and Columbia expired, Douglas decided to bring his business elsewhere. 'My father taught me,' Douglas explained, 'that a good business deal is one which is beneficial to both parties. In that sense the Columbia deal was not a good business deal. I discovered that I work best in a funky little office with just a reader and a secretary.' With his commitment to the studio finished, Michael was free to strike up a distribution deal for *Romancing the Stone* with 20th Century-Fox. And in 1983, he scored his ideal director: Robert Zemeckis.

Michael was a big fan of Robert Zemeckis's 1980 comedy *Used Cars*, which Zemeckis directed and co-wrote with Robert Gale. Featuring Kurt Russell, *Used Cars* was a good-naturedly tasteless saga of rival car dealers engaged in excessive sales pitch hijinks.

A USC film grad, Zemeckis broke into the industry by screening one of his student efforts for Steven Spielberg and John Milius, who, along with George Lucas, were also USC alumni. Their favourable reception led to Zemeckis's collaboration with Robert Gale on the screenplay of Spielberg's manic comedy monstrosity, *1941*, and his first major directorial effort, *I Wanna Hold Your Hand*.

In the three years after *Used Cars* came out, Zemeckis wasn't exactly deluged with offers; critics liked his films but audiences found them easy to resist. So when Michael Douglas asked Zemeckis to consider directing his new project, he didn't take long to decide. Three days later, the producer and his new director were Mexico-bound, scouting tropical locations for their adventure epic.

For the role of Ralph, the half-pint hood who tails Joan and Jack over hill and dale of Colombian countryside, Michael's selection of a paunchy, 'five-foot-tall, balding Italian guy from New Jersey' couldn't have been more perfect. Danny DeVito, a graduate of the American Academy of Dramatic Arts, caught Michael's eye in a 1971 off-Broadway revival of *One Flew Over the Cuckoo's Nest* (in the role of Anthony Martini). A few months later, Douglas cast DeVito in his film version of *Cuckoo's Nest.*

DeVito went on to gain notoriety as the taxi-dispatcher-you-love-to-hate, Louis DePalma of TV's popular 'Taxi'. But it was as *Romancing*'s long-suffering malevolent that he first showed his potential as an offbeat screen personality.

For the part of Joan Wilder, mousy-novelist-turned-adventuress, Douglas was still fishing. He approached several actresses and even visited the *Terms of Endearment* set in a futile attempt to coax Debra Winger into taking the part. Then 20th Century-Fox production president Joe Wizan suggested a beautiful young actress who'd recently debuted opposite William Hurt as *Body Heat*'s sizzling *femme fatale* – a blonde, twenty-nine-year-old, 5 foot 8 inch actress named Kathleen Turner.

Hailing from Springfield, Missouri, Ms Turner was the third of four children born to a consul in the American diplomatic service. Kathleen spent her formative years in such exotic locales as Cuba and Venezuela, where she developed keen artistic interests, unlike her more academically oriented siblings. Tackling dance in the fifth grade, Kathleen became impassioned by theatre after moving to London at the age of thirteen. 'It set me on fire,' she recalled.

Despite Dad's opposition to a theatre career, Kathleen

enrolled as a drama student at the University of Maryland, and went on to strengthen her craft on the set of NBC's daytime soap, 'The Doctors'. Replacing Kathryn Harrold, who held the role from 1976 to '78, Kathleen played avaricious seductress Nola Dancy Aldrich and was a mainstay on the show from 1978 to '79.

Following her captivating dramatic performance as *Body Heat*'s Matty Walker, Kathleen demonstrated her comedic range in *The Man With Two Brains* by doing a send-up of the temptress parts she'd thus far portrayed. But to land the part of Steve Martin's goldfish-torturing bitch-wife, Kathleen said she 'had to get in there and knock them out. I fell on my face and crawled up Steve Martin's leg, and then finally they said, "It's yours!" '

Ms Turner's name first arose in conjunction with *Romancing the Stone* when, at a casting meeting, Joe Wizan mentioned the gorgeous actress who happened to pick up a set of keys at his home the previous day. After reading the script, Kathleen was called to California to meet Michael.

'It was your typical kind of meeting in the producer's office,' said Kathleen of the encounter. 'I think I had on a short skirt. I figure my legs are my best asset so I try to use them. Michael had talked to all the people I'd worked with because one of the major considerations was living with a supposedly temperamental actress-type female in the jungles of Mexico for three months.'

At first, Michael wasn't completely sold on Ms Turner. 'All I knew at the time was that sultry vamp quality,' Michael recalled, and he feared she might be 'too much woman' to fill Joan Wilder's dowdy shoes. But their first meeting was encouraging and her screen test quelled all his doubts. 'She showed us she was a consummate actress,' Michael declared, and he was ready to whisk her off to Mexico where the truly problematic aspects of the production would soon manifest themselves.

Location shooting in Mexico started in July of '83. Mexico had been selected over Colombia for expediency's sake (it was closer to California and less expensive), but it turned into a nightmare for Douglas's hardy crew. 'This was a linear chase film,' explained Douglas. 'Every day there was a different location' – and consequently, a new set of problems.

For four months they traipsed about Mexico, roaming from their warehouse-turned-studio in Mexico City, to the cliffs of Xico, and the fortress at San Juan de Ulua. Often they'd spend weeks at a time shooting in isolated rural areas such as Barraca Grande's narrow mountain roads. 'We were so far from medical facilities,' remembered Zemeckis, 'we didn't just have a nurse like most productions – we had a full-fledged doctor on the set at all times.'

There were several close calls in the course of shooting. 'One storm was so violent, it caused a mud slide that trapped us on top of a winding mountain road in Xalapa,' reported Douglas. 'Another slide sent mud crashing down on Kathleen and several members of the crew. Miraculously, no one was seriously hurt.'

Robert Zemeckis remembered almost being obliterated by an avalanche of mud in the first week of shooting. 'I walked out with the cameraman to a ledge overlooking the valley two hundred feet below after we finished a shot and shouted, "That's a wrap." We heard a huge roar and suddenly the mountain behind us gave way. We were in an ocean of mud. I looked up to see a giant rock hanging there above us.' As Zemeckis recalled there was nothing in the script about the crew getting crushed by a boulder in a sea of wet dirt, so he deemed it necessary for everyone to hightail out of the precarious situation.

This superfluity of regional precipitation was easily

explained: Douglas's production had arrived at the height of the rainy season. Locals assured the film crew that although it was rainy season, they needn't worry – it would only rain daily for around a half hour at twilight and then stop. But contrary to native meteorological forecasts, it rained and rained and *rained*; the region ended up with more rainfall than it had seen in the past thirty-five years.

Douglas would arrive at previously scouted locations to find rivers and lakes had sprung up where before there was dry land. Sometimes bridges had to be built just to *get* to locations. But no matter what the weather gods threw at them, 'Michael seemed to be on top of every situation,' said Kathleen Turner. 'If a road washed out and we couldn't get to our location, the next morning there were thirty dump trucks full of gravel waiting to lay in that road. We were building Douglasland all through Mexico.' Then at the end of a day's shooting, tractors would tow the semis out of the mud like giant sleds, just so everybody could return home.

Initially, Zemeckis was almost pleased by the incessant downpours pelting the company since many scenes called for storms and generally moist conditions . . . until he realised that real rain doesn't photograph like *real* rain. Nor could he turn it on and off as he wished. 'We ended up having to make all our own rain for the scenes,' Zemeckis complained. 'We'd get all wet and miserable waiting for the real rain to stop so we could start our phoney rain.'

Plagued by tropical storms, mud slides, heat waves, and the need for constant mobility as demanded by the script, the capper of Douglas's mad expedition was four weeks spent in the sweltering jungles of El Arsenal. Danny DeVito remembered thinking it was like being in the middle of 'a Bosch painting'.

Two to three weeks of shooting were spent on a sequence that, after editing, filled a mere forty-five seconds of screen time

– the famous 'mudslide' scene. As it appears in the movie, the action consists of Jack Colton tossing Joan Wilder's suitcase over the side of a mountain road. Before Joan has a chance to protest, the ground beneath them gives way. They plummet down the mountainside, tumbling in a roaring river of mud and foliate debris. Joan lands in a pond of filthy water at the foot of the mountain, drenched in slime, but relatively unscathed. Colton is propelled into the mire seconds afterwards, landing with a splash smack dab, and face down, between her legs.

This was the clip that Michael used to hype the film. The brief sequence was a perfect teaser, encapsulating the idea that the film was 'fun.' But it wasn't much fun for the stunt people who repeatedly underwent the torturous ride. Jeannie Epper, Kathleen Turner's double for *Romancing*, described the memorable sequence as 'unbelievably difficult – physically and mentally.' Epper, a veteran stuntwoman, had doubled for Angie Dickinson, Lynda Carter, Shirley MacLaine, Shelley Long, and Linda Evans (ever since her *Big Valley* days). She earned $50,000 for her work on *Romancing the Stone* and was awarded 1984's Most Spectacular Stunt Award for the mud slide scene, but almost didn't survive to collect either. 'A couple of times I flipped upside down and nearly drowned in mud. Then I'd have to clean up, dry off, change clothes and do it again.'

Douglas remembered, 'Poor [Jeannie] was beat to hell. She'd come back crying, "I can't do it again." We had two hundred gallons of water that we'd dump behind the stunt people into a trough. It would hit them in the back . . . and they'd just take off. We had to have cargo nets in place every once in a while so they could grab on to something. They couldn't do the whole fall – it would kill them.'

Epper's *Romancing the Stone* contract stipulated that in case she got injured in the course of duty, she would be transported, via Lear jet, to a US hospital of her choice. 'I was more trusting when I was younger because I knew everyone,' explained Epper. 'Now I work with so many people I don't know, it's necessary to double check everything.'

As for his own spectacular dive into Kathleen Turner's crotch, Douglas preened, 'It requires some expertise to dive between a lady's legs, close enough but not too far away.'

Kathleen had her hands full contending with mud, inclement weather, and her producer/co-star hurtling himself at her nether regions. It can be downright confusing when your romantic lead also happens to be your boss. 'Kathleen was a real trouper down there,' praised Douglas. 'It's not always easy working with an actor who's also the producer.' Zemeckis confirmed this, adding, 'At first I was a bit intimidated. I had to direct the boss. But Michael didn't bring his acting role into his producing role or vice versa.'

The point of view of an actor/producer is a mildly schizophrenic state of mind. Whereas an actor basically needs to withdraw from reality to focus on himself and pull his energies inwards, producers have to oversee a plethora of external details and spread their concentration over a vast arena of activities. 'In acting, you're paid to be selfish,' philosophised Michael. 'Producing, you have to have three hundred and sixty degree vision. I don't know if producing affects my acting; I know it makes acting less fun.'

It's a wonder Michael didn't go genuinely schizoid on the set from trying to concentrate on emoting with Kathleen Turner, while just behind the camera a dozen frantic crew members lined up waiting to announce the latest catastrophes. 'I underestimated the logistics of shooting a chase adventure in the jungle,' Douglas said of the whole affair. 'We were flying without a net.'

The four-month endurance test of jungle film-making took

its toll on every member of cast and crew, not leastly the director and producer. Douglas was horrified to find himself shrivelling up and losing weight; Zemeckis emerged from the production twenty pounds lighter and a grizzled 'seen-it-all' veteran. Nine months after beginning his movie-making adventure with Douglas, Zemeckis was still unnerved by memories of nonstop toil and tribulation: 'It was hard on your mind, your clothes, your spirit, and your body. But I survived.'

When the jungle ordeal finally concluded, Douglas complained he was 'really fried', but there was to be no rest for the weary producer; the studio ordered a rush spring release for the picture. The bigwigs at Fox were presumably concerned about *Romancing* coming out well before *Indiana Jones and the Temple of Doom* (Spielberg's *Raiders of the Lost Ark* sequel). There'd already been too much advance buzz about *Romancing* being another *Raiders*, and the fact that Zemeckis was a former Spielberg protégé lent credence to the rumours.

Unlike *Raiders*, *Romancing* was a very contemporary story told from a woman's perspective. But in Zemeckis's opinion, even if he hadn't had close professional ties with Spielberg, it was inevitable that the differences between the films would be overlooked and comparisons drawn. 'Any movie that offers exotic locations and exciting action will be compared to *Raiders*,' Zemeckis asserted. 'There's nothing you can do about it. It's sort of an industry shorthand that allows people in this business to sell movies.'

Nevertheless, Michael gets p.o.'d when either *Romancing the Stone* or *Starman* are minimised by critics as rip-offs of Spielberg's *Raiders* or *ET*, respectively. 'The facts are that *Starman* was written before *ET*. I'd be happy to show people early drafts of *ET* and the dates when *Starman* came in. *Romancing* was written a year and a half before *Raiders of the Lost Ark*. Somebody should ask Steven [Spielberg] where it all comes from. But I do attribute *Raiders'* success for allowing *Romancing* to be made.'

A large part of *Romancing*'s success was due to Douglas's relentless plugging of the film. In promoting the movie a few things had to be borne in mind: it was not like the rest of Hollywood's crop of high concept, one-sentence plots that were favoured at the time – pictures like *Splash* or the miscellaneous teen-oriented dross. There was a little more stirring beneath the surface of Joan Wilder's adventure.

Also *Romancing*'s script combined several different types of plot elements, borrowing freely from romance, comedy, and action genres. Concisely communicating that array of styles could be difficult. It distinguished itself from the typical Hollywood thriller as a woman's adventure that utilised such twists as the heroine rescuing herself at the climax because the hero arrives too late.

Fortunately, Douglas had his forty-five-second mudslide clip to help convey the tongue-in-cheek derring-do attitude of the film, and he milked it for all its worth. Michael brought it to every national and local talk show and TV news magazine on the circuit. (On her show, Liz Smith complimented the clip as the best promo she'd ever seen.) Guest-hosting *Saturday Night Live*, he managed to slip it into the programme three times. After plugging it in his opening monologue, Michael promised the audience he wouldn't mention it again for the duration of the broadcast. Instead, Michael turned his back to the camera to reveal, boldly emblazoned on his satin jacket, the legend *Romancing the Stone*.

Romancing's positive reception soon invited industry chatterings of the old 'Revenge-of-the-Son-of–' routine, but for the moment, Michael insisted on putting any sequel plans on the back burner. 'My next picture,' he said, 'has to be a nice studio thing where at least you can get dried off between takes.'

Chapter Eight

A JEWEL IN THE MUD

'I think they should hire me out as a rain god.'

– Michael Douglas, '87

'My biggest pleasure with *Jewel* and *Romancing*, especially since I have a young son, is that they're pictures the whole family can enjoy. Everyone finds a different level. I also think one of the reasons why people would want to rent them or watch them on cable is because it's nice to find an opportunity where everyone can watch TV together rather than on their individual sets.'

– Michael Douglas, '87

'Acting is like being a child and producing is like being an adult. . . . It's a magical combination of activities.'

– Michael Douglas, '87

Towards the end of 1984, with *Romancing*'s publicity blitz nearing its saturation point, Michael decided he deserved to spend some time with his family. Rumours abounded, hinting at the instability of his marriage and blaming his long absences and intensive film production schedule. 'We did take a break from time to time,' admitted Michael, 'but there was never a formal separation.' While Michael toiled in Mexico, Diandra visited three times, bringing four-year-old Cameron with her to Via De Bravo where the 'fiesta scenes' were shot.

Diandra and Michael decided that a return to the East Coast would improve their situation. They settled in an expansive apartment overlooking Central Park West ('about six blocks from where I grew up,' according to Michael) just in time for Cameron to start school.

To balance professional and domestic demands, Michael sorted out a compromise allowing time for both: 'When I'm working, that's my priority, and when it's over, we spend time together. Of course [Diandra and Cameron] come visit me on the set. The big dilemma is that I love my work – it's very rewarding to me – so it's just a matter of finding time for a break.'

Other reasons for a 'rest' were work related – Michael was seeking new projects. 'There just don't seem to be the parts around,' he observed at the time. 'I love acting and I want to do more, but I can't find the roles and when I do there's always a lot of competition for them.' Besides this perennial actor's gripe, Michael's research for new productions also distracted him from finding the right roles.

If a film hits, the actor and director get swamped with offers and can glide more or less easily into the next proffered project. The producer must first land a solid script, and then gather backers, distribution, cast, etc. – an altogether time-consuming prospect. If one happens to be a producer/actor à la Douglas, venture hunting cuts into time that could otherwise be devoted to an acting agenda.

'One of the things I dislike about producing,' explained Douglas, 'is that it takes up so much time. When the movie works, it's rewarding to see your co-star being sought for another picture and have your director wanted for something else. As for the producer, unfortunately, it just means starting the struggle all over again.'

Reunited with scripting cohort Bob Gale, Bob Zemeckis scored tremendously with *Back to the Future*. Immediately after *Romancing*, Kathleen Turner began work on a controversial Ken Russell film. Most of *Crimes of Passion*'s controversy centred on her character's kinky encounters with a cop's billy club and a john's big toe. Kathleen's convincing rendition of part-time prostitute China Blue led her to coyly note, 'It's hard to act something as basic as sexual excitement without arousing it.'

Ms Turner's reputation with the critics was hardly sullied: *Time* magazine venerated her as 'the kind of treasure everybody in Hollywood should be filching a map to discover'; Richard Shickel declared her 'the movies' first authentically mysterious female presence since Garbo.' The *Village Voice*'s Andrew Sarris wrote: 'One might say that a star is born when one begins mentally casting her for everything in sight. So it is for me with Kathleen Turner at this moment in film history.' By 1986, Kathleen Turner ranked on the *Motion Picture Almanac*'s list of Top 10 box office champs.

Romancing the Stone made Kathleen Turner's career, while Douglas gained only moderate recognition; to be a producer/actor is to be a producer first, before and after the movie's done. As *Romancing* told the tale of a woman's growth, quite logically audience attention had to be drawn to Kathleen Turner. 'If we had screwed around with that,' explained Douglas, 'I wouldn't have made myself a star because maybe the picture would have been a turkey. Stars are made out of pictures that are successful.'

Nevertheless, Michael didn't wait long for his next role – Zach, the choreography director in *A Chorus Line*. Appearing in *A Chorus Line* offered several advantages to Michael at this juncture: he could remain in New York, work with Oscar-winning director Richard Attenborough, and the limited screen time Michael's character occupied left him sufficient spare time to pursue producíary interests.

Michael described Zach as 'someone who puts art before life. For him artistic creation is more important than any personal relationship.' Zach disdainfully lords over a group of anxious-to-please dancers who are auditioning for a place in the chorus line he's assembling. His manner is shrill, aggressive, and insensitive. 'He's a cold, obsessive guy,' said Douglas, 'who responds to a vision more than to people.' Simply put, 'He has bite.'

It took almost a decade for Broadway's record-setting dance/musical to make it onto film; at first, it looked as if it might never happen. The play won a Pulitzer Prize, and its original cast received nine Tony Awards. *A Chorus Line* was not only the longest continuously running show in Broadway history, but a favourite on national road shows as well.

Many directors and writers enlisted for the film adaptation were intimidated by the stage version's unchallenged appeal. Bo Goldman, co-scriptwriter of *One Flew Over the Cuckoo's Nest* tried to addend in his screenplay an unhappy love story ending involving principal characters Zach and Cassie (one of the dancers, played by Alyson Reed). Goldman's idea was rejected. According to Richard Attenborough, who took up the directorial gauntlet, directors 'felt that if they just filmed the play as is, they wouldn't get any credit. If they changed it radically, they could be accused of trashing a classic.' Casting the lead also proved difficult. Before settling on Michael Douglas, talents as diverse as Mikhail Baryshnikov and John Travolta were touted as the ideal Zach.

As usual, monetary disputes contributed to the delay. When, in 1976, Joseph Papp's New York Shakespeare Festival (which originally presented the play in its 299 seater in downtown

Manhattan) sold the rights to *A Chorus Line* for $5.5 million, a clause was appended requiring that the film remain unreleased for a minimum of five years. What's more, a profit-sharing agreement stipulated a substantial royalty (twenty per cent, more than double the standard play-to-film deal), to be deducted when the movie grossed over $30 million.

With prospects of a large investment combined with potentially inadequate returns looming over the play, the rights to *A Chorus Line* were resold many times. Eventually they ended up in the possession of Cy Feuer and Ernest Martin, the duo who'd first approached Papp to buy the rights while it was still in previews. Feuer and Martin then approved screenwriter Arnold Schulman (*Goodbye, Columbus*), the last of many writers to reshape the script.

Alterations, which by most accounts (including Attenborough's), enfeebled the screenplay, included the expanded dramatic function of Zach's strained relationship with Cassie, and insertion of multiple flashbacks to provide background to characters and events. Critics argued that these elaborations violated the minimalist aesthetic of the play, while serving virtually no narrative purpose or offering any new insights. Songs, choreography, and other production details were also either eliminated or compromised in the film version.

Attenborough halfheartedly defended his efforts, saying that although flashbacks and scene changes went against the original uninterrupted concept of the theatrical presentation, he was obliged to retain them to satisfy the producers and the storyline.

'Unfortunately, we couldn't do on film what is done in the play,' Attenborough observed, 'which is to play Zach in the back of the theatre and have his voice come from behind the audience's head. On film, that would have been the equivalent of a narrator, which would have been all wrong. So to balance our decision to show Zach sitting in the theatre we felt we had to balance that with showing more of Cassie from the stage.'

Whatever his excuses, Attenborough's *A Chorus Line* elicited from critics reactions no stronger than 'watchable,' 'decent' and 'middling'. Michael's performance was deemed a 'disappointment'.

Compared with his usual give-it-all-yer-gusto approach to filmmaking, Michael's participation in *A Chorus Line* did seem reserved. If Michael was disappointed in the way the movie turned out it isn't known, but another major project did weigh on his mind.

A mere two months after *Romancing*'s release, there'd been whispers of a sequel; but 20th Century-Fox, in the midst of administrative changes, decided no positive move would be made until they tallied all the figures generated by the film. In August of '84, Fox informed Douglas, 'We want a sequel and we need it pronto . . . by Christmas of '85.' Only one decisive obstacle blocked Douglas's path – he had no script.

Michael did have some loose ideas – mostly he wanted to avoid any plot that entailed excess rain or mud – and he started meeting with writers. Diane Thomas, *Romancing the Stone*'s creator, was under contract to Steven Spielberg. Searching for new blood, Michael randomly scanned odd scripts until he happened upon a writer that interested him; he'd then summon the writer for a bull session and bounce ideas off his noggin. Eventually, Michael settled on the combo of Mark Rosenthal and Lawrence Konner.

Together they assembled the story of Jack and Joan's epic desert trek with a charming holy man, known throughout the land as the 'jewel'. En route, the trio become embroiled in a politically motivated holy war, strike up an unlikely alliance with their old nemesis Ralph (Danny DeVito), and tangle with fanatics, assassins, camels, whirling dervishes, and bare-breasted Nubian tribeswomen. Somehow, Jack and Joan even manage to get married.

'It's tough doing a can-you-top-this-one movie,' affirmed co-producer Joel Douglas. 'We decided not to do a sequel in the classical Hollywood sense, but to take the main characters from *Romancing* and put them into a different life situation.'

Whereas *Romancing the Stone* dealt with Joan Wilder's growth and burgeoning self-confidence, *Jewel of the Nile*, Douglas explained, 'by contrast is about the growing up of Jack Colton . . . of the two as a couple. Colton is a guy who's always on the move. When the going gets rough, he's always ready to take off. He has to recognise just how much he loves this woman and what sacrifices he'd be willing to make.'

Jewel of the Nile's first draft, prepared by early November, got the green light from Fox's higher-ups, and Michael slaved over rewrites while shooting *A Chorus Line*. 'I converted a dressing room in the Mark Hellinger Theater [where the film was being shot] into an office. When the crew would go off to work on the dance numbers, I'd sit upstairs and work on the script. The last day of the picture we filmed all night and then I headed to the airport to catch an 8:30 a.m. flight to Morocco.'

Douglas chose Lewis Teague, former Roger Corman protégé (*Lady in Red*) and director of two Stephen King adaptations (*Cujo* and *Cat's Eye*) to direct the flick, because Zemeckis was unavailable. Douglas chose Zemeckis for *Romancing* because he admired the contemporary style of humour and high energy level displayed in his earlier works. For *Jewel*, Douglas wanted a 'fresh' director, but as it would be a massive production, he required someone with experience.

Michael remembered a campy flick he'd seen in which a pet baby alligator is flushed down a toilet. In the sewers it grows to monstrous proportions, ultimately emerging to terrorise Chicago in the aptly entitled *Alligator*. Michael was both amused and interested, and he noted director Lewis Teague's name in the credits.

Viewing *Cujo* Michael found himself scared and interested. He eventually learned that Teague pulled off *Cujo* with virtually no preparation, replacing a director who had already shot a week's worth of footage. Considering how effective the film was, Michael found Teague's ride to the rescue all the more impressive. These qualifications singled out Teague for what was to be Douglas's most epic undertaking to date.

Fresh from an all-night shoot in Manhattan, Douglas arrived in Morocco and immediately realised he 'was in deep shit'. At the Casablanca airport, he met Teague and the local production manager, who dashed around renting cars. It quickly dawned on Michael that these two guys comprised the full extent of his Moroccan crew; everyone else was in Nice, France. Why Nice? Michael recalled, 'The production man said, "Well, Nice is a good stepping off point." Stepping off point? It's a continent and three and a half jet hours away.'

Michael requested to be driven to his office. As it turned out, Michael neither had an office nor a chauffeur. 'I wasn't looking for an entourage,' Michael said, 'but it's pretty rough to have to drive your own car when you're producing a $20 million picture.' A day later, when Michael realised that the locations had not yet been firmed up, 'I went to my hotel room and just cried.'

Michael deliberated for about a day, pondering whether to reveal the extent of his disarray to the studio. With six weeks left till shooting, he knew further postponement meant that the schedule would spill over into the unbearable 100-degree-plus heat of the Moroccan summer. 'That was when I heard this screaming voice inside me shout, "Here you go. Life's been real good. You've been waiting for someone to do something really bad to you and this is it." '

Desperate, Michael phoned brother Joel and urged him, 'You get over here, immediately, the next plane. This is a disaster.' The sibling co-producer of many Michael Douglas presentations, Joel functioned as a reliable and trustworthy crutch in times of crisis. As *grand fromage*, Michael at all times tried to maintain an impression of omniscient control, but the enormous pressures entailed in making *Jewel* sometimes reduced him to behind-the-scenes frailty. 'I cried a lot,' confessed Michael, 'and hugged my brother.'

Michael and Joel's brotherly alliance also required Joel to cover the producer's back when he was busy acting. In Morocco, where the air was thick with financial and political arrangements and kickbacks, Joel kept quite adequately occupied.

Once the brothers scouted and organised all the location details, Michael flew to California to finish scripting and casting chores. No sooner back on solid ground, he learned that Kathleen Turner refused to do the film. Turner read the script's first draft and judged it below her standards; she'd also been offered a part she preferred in *The Money Pit*, an upcoming Spielberg production whose shooting schedule overlapped with *Jewel*. In response to Kathleen's refusal, 20th Century-Fox offered her an alternative: a $25 million lawsuit.

'It wasn't that I ever intended *not* doing the sequel,' explained Ms Turner. 'I just wanted *Jewel* to have the same quality as the original, and I felt that what I had been given was written in the wrong spirit. . . . Women writers are different than men. [The males] were writing jokes I didn't find funny, like having Africans drag Joan off into a hut.'

While Kathleen bears Michael no grudge, she remains bitter about the film industry's money madness; she argues that quality of product should be Hollywood's overriding aim but, 'they're only concerned with maintaining a business. I hope that the best of them want to make a good film; but the rest should be bank tellers.' When it comes to artistic control, be it sex scenes or any variety of script problem, Kathleen asserts that 'the only power an actor has is the ability to say no. You've got to hold onto that and not make decisions based on money or they own you.'

Douglas and Turner resolved their script differences, but Michael's troubles were far from finished. About a week before attending the Academy Award ceremonies, Michael received word that his production designer, location manager, and their pilot had died in a plane crash. 'They were missing for four days,' Michael recalled. 'It was hard for everybody. I didn't know whether to go over there. My brother was telling me, "We're doing everything we can, you've got to keep going ahead with the script. There's nothing you can do here." But it was a very, very sad and uncomfortable time, trying to continue with the picture, having meetings, and you kind of drift off for a while and look out the window, and out there somewhere they're still missing.'

Jewel of the Nile's toll had begun to surpass predictable movie-making expenditures; Michael felt like he was 'going against the gods.' After the tragic loss of their fellow crew members, some of the company wished to leave, believing the picture was doomed. But Michael relentlessly ploughed ahead, steeling himself for the final test of his produciary mettle – the filming itself.

Returning to Morocco, he found that the prearranged crew accommodations were inadequate and requested that members of the production double up. When the English crew members refused, Michael blew his top. He called the head of production at Fox (who had a mutual agreement with Douglas about the production manager) and railed about the unreasonable situation. The production manager and all other troublesome crew members were promptly dismissed. 'I cleaned house,' Michael tersely explained.

Though the rabble-rousers were purged from the camp, complications perpetually afflicted the shoot. Two thousand posters and flags that had been readied for a mass rally had to be destroyed and rewritten just hours before shooting. Unbeknownst to the production crew, the Arabic phrase they'd utilised translated to a sacrilegious pronouncement. The climax, staged in the city of Mekne's Royal Square, transformed the fourteen-thousand-square-foot yard enclosure into the holy city of Khadir. But because the forty-foot-high palace walls were treasured antiquities, they couldn't be pierced with nails or otherwise mutilated, not even to stabilise props in the chaotic scene. A web of ladders, ropes, and cranes latticed around the set ultimately resolved the dilemma.

Production designer Terence Smith spent seven weeks in the desert building a set in an area which had been drought-stricken for six years. Just as he finished constructing one and a half miles of castle walls, bridges, and road, rain deluged the spot for eight days, a local record. 'If this had happened two thousand years ago,' lamented Smith, 'it would have gotten in the Bible. Something in the Atlas mountains gave way and a wall of water eight feet high swept down through the dry river bed. In fifteen seconds everything had been washed away.'

Nearly all props and movie-making equipment were imported, but getting them through customs and onto the set proved a monumental hassle; red tape enveloped every shipment down to basic nuts and bolts. Before Douglas could import ersatz weaponry into the country (including Uzi machine guns from Israel, technically an enemy of Morocco) approval had to be officiated by a military tribunal personally established by King Hassan II. Unable to shoot realistic battle scenes with rubber guns, a bureaucratic bog threatened to submerge the production. What's more, Douglas and crew were in danger of losing their questionable accommodations.

Michael flipped out. Flying to the capital city of Rabat, and to Marrakesh (home of the king's forty-two palaces), he tracked down the responsible government officials and issued a chilling ultimatum: 'You know "Good Morning America"?' he demanded. ' "Good Morning America" is going to have their crews out to watch us get kicked out of our offices and hotel.' The threat of ugly international press was the only thing that really scared the Arab bureaucracy. Michael got his guns.

Michael also brought in a full-scale replica of an American F-16 fighter jet (capable of firing real missiles) he'd commissioned from a team of British and French special effects experts at La Victorinne Studios in Nice. At a cost of a quarter of a million dollars and four months' effort, the model was so accurate, according to Joel Douglas, that only an expert's first-hand inspection could reveal its flightless traits.

It remains unknown what reaction Algeria, Morocco's militant neighbour, had to the delivery of an apparent warplane at a Moroccan airbase in minute proximity to their shared border, but the jet arrived without a hitch.

The Arab version of Lent, Ramadan, was greeted by the beleaguered *Jewel* cast with something less than enthusiasm. A month-long celebration calling for daily fasting and nightly hooplah,* it inconveniently coincided with shooting of the film's climactic rally. Ramadan's topsy-turvy scheduling motivated some astute second-guessing from the production staff (dubbed by some sardonic studio executives as the 'Jews of the Nile')

*For the duration of Ramadan, Muslims abstain from food, drink, smoking and sexual activities from sunrise till sunset. At 8:30 p.m. a cannon booms and the famished populace emerge to roam the streets, eating voraciously and igniting firecrackers. Just before dawn, all Muslims partake of a large feast before turning in for the night.

as to the possible behaviour of their 2,500 two-dollar-a-day Arab extras.

Confounding cultural interaction reached its zenith on the shoot when Teague and Douglas at one point discovered they couldn't find a common language between themselves, a Senegalese dance troupe (representing Nubians), and a Guinean actor (playing their chief). Except for one of Teague's assistants and a government rep from the cultural centre, none of Douglas's crew spoke a speck of Arabic. The Guinean chief spoke neither English, French, nor Senegalese; the Senegalese spoke French, but couldn't translate to the Berber-fluent Guinean. After a prolonged and unresolved bout of multilingual babble, Teague and Douglas gave up. 'I don't think there's a way to get from here to there,' Michael shrugged.

Morocco's beasts of burden conspired to contribute their fair share of abuse. Danny DeVito, on Dr Ruth Westheimer's show,* reminisced about troubled negotiations with his reticent steed, 'Humphrey' the camel. When DeVito first approached the disdainful animal, his amicable advances met with a discouraging reproof; eyeing Danny dubiously, Humphrey spewed forth a formidable wad of camel mucus. Once this distasteful baptism broke the ice, DeVito and Humphrey settled into an uneasy partnership. DeVito never quite adjusted to camel riding though; he characterised the rides as simultaneously 'bumpy' and 'sexual'.

Whereas *Romancing the Stone* took Michael and company about five and a half to six years to complete, *Jewel of the Nile*, an ambitiously massive production, concluded relatively quickly – especially considering the brain-boggling array of problems the production faced. By the end of *Jewel's* five-month shoot, temperatures had soared to 130 degrees and the food and

*Broadcast February 3, 1988, on the Lifetime cable channel.

accommodations were lousy. Sunstroke, dysentery, cholera, and hepatitis ran rampant among crew members, almost necessitating a full-scale quarantine.

The true high point of the entire experience probably wasn't the night the cast assembled to watch a specially imported videotape of the Celtics-Lakers basketball playoff; it more likely came the day they finally left Morocco. 'When we finished up,' Michael fondly remembers, 'I brought down a C-136 transport plane and a 737. We just opened up the transport's mouth and drove up with our trucks, crane, everything, hopped on the 737 and landed in France. That was one of the nicest moments, knowing we were headed for France.'

Michael and Joel travelled on to London to edit the film and work on the soundtrack. Five weeks remained to write, record, and complete the soundtrack music before the uncompromising deadline of final edit arrived. With the limited time at their disposal, Michael monopolised time at England's Battery Studios' multitrack recording facilities. For African-styled background music, engineers digitally sampled a wide range of native sounds and fed them into a Fairlight computerised synthesiser. Michael sat in the control room and could personally select exactly whatever sound he desired for any given scene.

Another product of his sessions at Battery Studios was the Billy Ocean tune, 'When the Going Gets Tough, the Tough Get Going'. Encapsulating the theme of the movie, this song itself became number one, selling over four million copies worldwide.

Compared to the all-out combat he'd waged in Morocco, Michael's endeavours at Battery turned out to be a civilised breeze; two days ahead of deadline, the soundtrack tapes were all ready for the final cut.

* * *

Jewel of the Nile and *A Chorus Line* had virtually simultaneous release dates in early December; no longer overshadowed by co-star Kathleen Turner, Michael Douglas faced the opposite predicament of being overexposed. Unlike *A Chorus Line*, *Jewel* could hardly be considered an unpopular film but critics generally greeted it with a raspberry.

The *Los Angeles Times*'s Michael Wilmington bemusedly condemned *Jewel* as 'another example of the dread Hollywood disease *chronic sequelitis*: last year's hit soufflé turning into this year's gaseous smorgasbord.' Compared to *Romancing*, *Jewel* boasted 'twice the action, twice the spectacle – and half the buoyancy, half the wit. Perhaps the new title should have been *Seducing the Boulder*.'

Gene Siskel offered a round of denunciations, and concluded that for depth of character, the film makers substituted the antics of 'camel jockeys and nomadic hordes.' The *Los Angeles Times* concurred, noting that 'somewhere in the background of this movie, you always seem to be hearing someone yell: "Bring on more elephants. Crash another plane! More dynamite on the left! Where's my mountain, for heaven's sake? It's 3 o'clock already!" '

With *Jewel of the Nile* ensconced in seemingly perpetual HBO rotation, suggestions of the inevitable sequel to the sequel have been broached. Michael has announced his eagerness to undertake the third chapter of Jack and Joan's continuing saga, and hinted that it would transpire in relatively 'civilised' surroundings for a change, such as Paris or Rome.

While waffling on a definite commitment, Kathleen Turner has promised to consider another instalment of the tale after completing her ongoing projects. However, she does harbour severe reservations: 'There's a lot more temptation now having found such a popular character as Joan, to keep the public's love for you by sticking closer to that sort of character. But that's boring. That's entrapment.' By the same token, Kathleen also reckons that 'should I overstep the boundaries of what people will accept from it, it could be very comforting to go back and do Joan.'

Reportedly, Danny DeVito has given a definite commitment, but true to his character Ralph, he was quoted in *Celebrity Plus* to the effect that he'd do a sequel 'only if Michael forks over enough cash.'

Chapter Nine

THE LOUDEST ATTRACTION

'. . . people don't come up and tell *me* their stories. Thank God. A shrink, I'm not.'

– Michael Douglas, '88

Fatal Attraction's contributions to Hollywood history are manifold: It contributed to the revitalisation of the multigenerational format by creating a buzz which pulled in moviegoers of all ages, its strong moral message neatly coincided with public sentiment and AIDS-related 'hysteria', and it made a hell of a lot of money.

Fatal Attraction's contributions to Douglas's history are also manifold: It put him on the front page of everything in print, he became one of those celestial types who are 'in demand', and it probably made him a hell of a lot of money.*

Certainly the nation was in need of a new approach to what constituted 'potential box office', as gangs of writers reeled drunkenly around their West Coast habitats, desperately trying to evolve one more flimsy plot involving naked female teenagers. 'We're getting away from the idea that kids only go to see

*Mr Douglas continues to evade discussion of tacky financial matters.

movies about kids, adults only go to see movies about adults,' explained Lindsay Doran, a senior VP of production at Paramount Studios. '*Stand By Me* proved that grown-ups will go to a movie about a twelve-year-old, and *Fatal Attraction* that kids will go to movies about adults.' The fact that both movies were financial mega-hits seems to have swayed the larger studios' inclinations to deliver product which neatly encapsulates some marketing research department's idea of what the people want.

For those not already in the know, *Fatal Attraction* is the woeful tale of a young, rising attorney, Dan Gallagher (Michael Douglas) who, along with his loving wife Beth (Anne Archer), his small child, and his dog, is tortured unrelentingly by weekend fling Alex Forrest (Glenn Close).

The sounds of a million salesmen mentally swearing off chance encounters of the close kind resounded through the halls of theatres, accompanied by the equally noisy 'I told you' looks emanating from wives and girlfriends. Not to mention the actual talk. People left the movie talking, and according to most sources, a large portion continued talking about *Fatal Attraction* for hours or days afterward. Furthermore, the effect of *Fatal Attraction* can be judged by the fact that the phrase itself became synonymous with a certain type of human condition.

Audience identification worked strongly in the movie's favour as well. 'The phenomenon that seems to be working is that [the movie] hits so close to home. I guess we've all known characters like [Alex Forrest] . . . where it comes to a point when you realise that anything you say to them will have no effect . . .' said director Adrian Lyne.

Michael remarked, 'I've never before been involved in a picture that emotionally hits people like this. . . . Women are dragging their boyfriends or their husbands to see it. It's sort of unrelenting.'

Fatal Attraction became the primo buzz word of 1987, polarising movie audiences all over the country and generating endless streams of cocktail party yap. Multidimensional postulations concerning its characters, plot, morality, and manipulative aspects drifted across the pages of every type of magazine. Those in 'the biz' couldn't stop commenting on its vocal audience. The screaming and cat-calling issuing from normally quiet sectors amazed even the film's actors and director. 'I wasn't prepared for how much of an audience-participation movie it was going to be,' Adrian Lyne told the *Los Angeles Times*.

'They're going nuts in the theatres. . . . People scream, they get hysterical. This is what making movies is all about,' Michael effused in *USA Today*.

Psychological circles quickly pinpointed *FA*'s divide and conquer tactics, its ability to separate men and women and personify the freefloating mistrust which often hovers between the sexes. One could almost hear the audience's thoughts: 'Men, God, they're all alike; they only think about one thing and they don't care about the consequences.' 'Women, you can't trust them, you never know what they're thinking. . . . Look what the crazy bitch is doing to that poor guy . . .'

While some simply ingested the story's basic premise of right and wrong, with Close playing Wicked Witch of the West to Douglas and Archer's Toto and Dorothy, others found Close's role offensive. Roger Ebert would later explain (when he picked *FA* as the year's Worst Oscar nomination) that one of his main objections to the film was the progressive deterioration and narrowing of Close's character. She begins as a rather interesting, complex woman and degenerates into a Saturday matinee maniac. Mr Ebert wasn't the only person to point out that Ms Close's rebound out of the tub is reminiscent of Jason of *Friday the Thirteenth* fame. Many single, career-oriented women were likewise upset by the suggestion that wives are *good* and unmarried women with jobs are *bad.** A faction of the male population also considered this demarcation dangerous.

Adrian Lyne doesn't agree with those who finger *FA* as antifeminist dogma, and he likewise discounts the theory that audiences see Douglas's character as blameless or vindicated. 'Both characters are tainted,' he told the *Los Angeles Times* in October of 1987. 'The only innocent in the picture is Anne. . . . I think the audience had a great deal of sympathy with Glenn. It lasted far into the second act.'

To its credit, the movie brought attention to the consequences of *l'amour fou* and its hideous effects on the lives of its perpetrators and victims. Stories in an issue of *People* magazine detailed the nightmares of men and women subjected to the insane whims of unbalanced suitors. When a panel of similar victims brought their ordeals to the 'Phil Donahue Show', an attitude engendered by the movie did surface, namely a feeling that they 'did something' to deserve whatever happened to them. But there was a definite increase in audience sympathy as these people told their stories, both for the recipients of these unbalanced affections and the unfortunate souls tangled in the madness of obsessive love. Some cases were the result of very limited initial contact between harasser and harassee, with no sexual contact whatsoever. Because these cases have come into the open, people are beginning to understand that the black and white stance of the movie is not real; there are extenuating circumstances and grey tones. In the real world, Michael Douglas's character could have been subjected to the same single-minded wrath even if he kept his pants on.

Another valuable aspect of *Fatal Attraction* is its portrayal of the hardships suffered by the hounded party when they try to deal with the problem through the authorities. The police's

*If one subscribes to this line of thought, it is also interesting to note that Close's character sports the masculine moniker 'Alex.'

position is unfortunate; harassment is a difficult charge to prove. But often, members of the law enforcement community, as well as people in general, take an unsympathetic attitude towards the victims. This produces an effect similar to the much-publicised horrors which women are still confronted with when trying to prove a charge of rape.

Fatal Attraction also managed to polarise its participants. 'I didn't sympathise with Glenn Close at all, her character too aggressively sought out a married man,' Anne Archer told *USA Today*. 'She set out to grab him, even though she'd seen me, his wife.' Michael Douglas presented a different, but no less personal view of the film's situation: 'There have been times . . . when I've had to deal with innuendo or rumour that I was involved with somebody who I may never have even known. It's hard, too, on my family. A couple of times I've tracked somebody down and followed up on it.' Producer Sherry Lansing adds, 'Very few people haven't called someone in the middle of the night to see if they're where they're supposed to be. I have.'

And Glenn Close echoed the refrain of Alex Forrest when she told Barbara Walters, 'I've gone through relationships where I was suffocated with desire . . . and you think you're going to die.'

Thought to be the ultimate AIDS cautionary fable because of its uncompromising condemnation of infidenlity, *Fatal Attraction*'s extremities managed to capitalise on America's AIDS-related unease/paranoia without mentioning the dread disease. Herein probably lies its ability to be both grim, depressing, *and* a blockbuster. Apparently, AIDS itself is too controversial and frightening to bring audiences rushing into movie theatres, and its uncontrollable spread makes the 'happy ending' impossible, so it must be personified and therefore rendered controllable. In this way, *FA* is comparable to the 1956 horror film, *Invasion of the Body Snatchers*, which used pods from space that duplicated a person's body so an alien mind could claim it, as an allegory for the feared spread of Communism, which supposedly sapped people of their free will in a similar fashion. The refrain then was the same, if you consider the quality that the disease and the cold-war view of Communism have in common – you can't necessarily see it, but it's there. Alex Forrest's initially deceptive appearance as a normal woman who blossoms into a full-fledged psychopath plays on the same phobia. On this level, Glenn Close's portrayal is extremely effective, especially when interacting with Douglas's character.

Michael Douglas's rendition of Dan Gallagher is the pinnacle of one of Michael's specialities which he dumped unceremoniously in *Romancing the Stone* and *Jewel of the Nile*. In *Fatal Attraction*, Michael is the quintessential poor schmuck, tossed hither, thither, and yon by events seemingly beyond his control. In *Running* he overcomes obstacles by hard labour and brains; a combination of the good old American work ethic and good old American ingenuity. In *FA*, he tries to kill the obstacle, but in the end his wife has to do it for him.

Certain astute observers elaborated on the horror/thriller angle, labelling it the first 'yuppie slasher' flick. Reflecting on other aspects of the violence displayed in *FA*, an LA citizen commented, 'If you look at the surface of the film, it says that the couple that kills together, stays together. It's the ultimate yuppie-fascist film.' This type of reaction probably came from the faction who housed the sneaking suspicion that *FA*'s characters weren't as concerned with the threat to their person as they were with the threat to their lifestyle.

Michael became interested in the central issues addressed in *Fatal Attraction* when he read a book by Gloria Nagy called *Virgin Kisses* which explored similar territory. As the story goes, he encountered Stanley Jaffe on an aeroplane, and the two spent some time comparing projects and shop talk. The initial reception to *Fatal Attraction* wasn't enthusiastic, partially because of some difficulty generating sympathy for the character of Dan Gallagher. Eventually, this simple chat turned into a more serious discussion, which included Sherry Lansing, Jaffe's co-producer who'd worked with Michael at several different companies and is one of his biggest supporters in the industry.

Michael worked with his producers to fashion a script which would appeal to the powers that be. Sherry felt justifiably confident in Michael's ability to make invaluable contributions, because of his background in production and his all-over experience. Another important factor in Michael's favour was his 'Nice-Guy' persona, which could possibly counterbalance the problems concerning the male lead's ability to win an audience over in spite of his actions.

One major sticking point which refused to go away had the mainstays of the production in a tailspin from the first drafts of the script until post-release leading to the infamous 'double-ending' fiasco. It could have been worse. Originally, there were nine different endings being considered. Basically, some critics objected to the fact that after a preview showing of the original ending, which had Close kill herself off à la *Madame Butterfly* out of camera sight, the audience strongly indicated that they wanted to see her die. Preview audiences also expressed displeasure at the resolve; Dan is blamed for the 'murder', but is saved in the nick of time by his wife.

In the era of 'money-talks' Hollywood, when it becomes more and more important to pull in big bucks, it's almost impossible to debate the issues raised by a production company's decision to change its product to suit the market. Suffice it to say, it happens occasionally, and the unwelcome attention garnered by *FA*'s switch probably had something to do with the amount of money it raked in. Japanese distributors considered using the original ending; 'Older people, especially women, prefer the original ending,' explained marketing manager Kiri Inomatta. 'It has more quality. But young people these days are sort of insensitive to arty types of movies.' Several European distributors, including the British faction, chose to keep the suicide finale.

Both endings broke box office records, and whichever way you see it, *Fatal Attraction* certainly had a desirable effect on its three stars' careers. Glenn Close, who'd won an Oscar nomination for her portrayal of Garp's mother in *The World According to Garp* and kudos for her part in the ensemble piece *The Big Chill*, wasn't even considered initially. She pushed hard for a chance to audition with Douglas. 'When Glenn made it known she was prepared to test, I became fascinated with the idea of using her,' Adrian Lyne told *People* magazine. 'She's a person you'd least expect to have this passion and irrational obsession. When she and Michael tested, an extraordinary erotic transformation took place. She was this tragic, bewildering mix of sexuality and rage – I watched Alex come to life.' Other actresses who tried but failed included Cheryl Ladd, Kirstie Alley, Melanie Griffith, Jacqueline Bisset, and Mimi Rodgers. Debra Winger turned it down.

Initally Jaffe couldn't see Close as Alex, perhaps because the character was visualised as somewhat younger in its first phases of development, but he came around after a brief reading. Close then consulted three separate psychiatrists in search of her character. When her homework couldn't provide the amount of anger called for, director Lyne claims, 'she would cry and she would scream at me. The script was shit! She was shit! The rage would turn into tears, and then she would be extraordinary. Like she had shaken off the layers.'

Ms Close also drew from her personal feelings and assessments of male/female relationships. 'Too many women define themselves in terms of a man. Look at me. In my marriages I was like an ameoba.' Glenn's two marriages, an early union with guitarist Cabot Wade and a much later one to financial big shot James Marias both failed, the latter sinking sometime during the filming of *Fatal Attraction.* This real-life emotional upheaval must have fueled Ms Close's effective performance in some way, for the audience reaction to her is simply too overwhelming to chalk up to your basic good performance. It is also interesting to note Close's own echoes of one of the film's basic premises. 'Men blossom under the nurturing of a good woman, while women don't often get that benefit from a man. I think of men and women as different species. Katharine Hepburn said they should live next door and visit each other once in a while. Not a bad idea.' Almost to prove her point, Ms Close decided not to wed John Starke, the father of her baby. The two retain separate, but nearby residences in New York City. This, plus her torrid sex scenes with Douglas, made her the focus of many supermarket magazines' front-page revelations, something which may have surprised the actress as much as any other result of the film.

Another participant who profited from a role in *Fatal Attraction* is Anne Archer, who played Michael's long-suffering wife. Ms Archer is the offspring of actor John Archer and actress Marjorie Lord (best remembered for 'The Danny Thomas Show'). Raised in LA, Anne's early exposure to the business imbued her with an inclination towards the bright lights, but until *Fatal Attraction*'s attention-garnering performance, Ms Archer's career was marred by forgettable films and failed television efforts. Starting in 1970 with minor movie parts, Anne worked her way 'up' to co-starring status in ill-fated endeavours like *Hero At Large* with John Ritter. The little box in America's living room proved equally unkind, for she endured two cancelled series and a no-go pilot. This led her to the conclusion that 'my career was pretty dead. I had such a rough time of it. I'd put off having kids with Terry [Jastrow, her second husband, an ABC Sports producer], waiting every year, thinking, "I'm going to get that big movie – things are going to open up for me." But at a certain point I said, "This is crazy," so I went ahead and got pregnant.'

After witnessing her mother's professional dismissal post-Danny Thomas, Ms Archer knew better than to trust the fickle attentions of the movie industry. Overlooked for many desirable projects, Anne returned to acting simply 'because I needed to earn some money.' In 1985, she latched onto a visible position on prime-time soap 'Falcon Crest,' paving the way for her successful audition for *Fatal Attraction*. Adrian Lyne says he chose Anne as an alternative to 'the cliché of the grey stay-at-home wife.' The fact that Michael Douglas admits that he's harboured 'a crush' for the sexy actress must have worked in her favour as well.

Even before her Oscar nomination, Anne Archer's performance brought her more attention than she'd ever expected. Reportedly, Archer's agent fielded 'zillions' of offers for television projects to accommodate preferable big-screen possibilities. The winner of the *Premiere* magazine's 1987 Reader's Poll for Best Supporting Actress stated that because of *FA*, 'I'm suddenly getting many more offers, but it hasn't meant the struggle is any less. I'm still competing for roles – only the group I'm competing against has changed.' She admitted her surprise at *Fatal Attraction*'s staggering success. 'None of us thought it would be a blockbuster – although I always did think it would push everybody's buttons.'

Button-pushing seems to be quite the catch phrase among the cast and crew of *FA*, or as producer Jaffe sometimes says, 'We didn't set out to make a heavy message picture, but it has touched a chord.' Whatever they set out to do, a heavy message picture is what they made, with the Oscar-nominated director Adrian Lyne playing a major part in some of the more subtle aspects of the movie's single-mindedness.

An oft-sensationalised but under-analysed aspect of *FA* is the outcome of the ensemble's determination to drive home their point without regard for details or the predictability of certain set-up gestures, or attention to conventional morals dictating the strength of on-screen sexuality. For instance, when the Gallaghers' child suddenly develops a yen for a pet rabbit, it becomes increasingly obvious that the rabbit must die. Like many successful films, *FA* holds onto its main-line objective and doesn't try to confuse the audience with a lot of subplots. Think of it as 1987–88's version of *Top Gun*, and it's easy to see why the majority of the audience couldn't care less about its antifeminist aspects, just as previous audiences ignored *Top Gun*'s war-mongering.

The film's frank sexuality underlines the horrific nature of the relationship between Alex and Dan. One can no longer dismiss Dan (or subsequently, Douglas) as a wimp after watching his sinkside grapple with Ms Close, who likewise looks as if she were trying to swallow him alive. This also underlines the aura of mistrust between the sexes previously mentioned – the couple is 'making love' with hatred, their emotions run the gamut from one extreme to the other. Close offers brutal love, while Archer offers safe marital love. Though they were held up as excessive, the movie's sex scenes are some of the more essential ones filmed in recent years, when gratuitous sex runs rampant in the business. This is the sort of thing that director Adrian Lyne excels in, as witnessed in the graphic and controversial *9½ Weeks*. The honesty of Close and Douglas's performances is disarming; it presents the somewhat ugly side of human sexuality in a way that's difficult to ignore.

Basically slotted into a reactive role for the majority of the film, Douglas really comes into his own during those steamy bedroom/kitchen moments. Without them, his later transformation into a man driven to raving lunacy wouldn't wash. The transformation of this mild-mannered lawyer into a hitherunseen (in this film or any other) cavemannish beast who expresses himself in such an uninhibited bodily fashion sent women home wondering what it was really like to have sex with Michael Douglas. *Fatal Attraction* not only established Michael as an actor to contend with, it made him into a true sex symbol, an aura he would continue to cultivate, though more obliquely, in *Wall Street*.

The big question though, is how did Michael attain that air of marital familiarity with the very sexual Anne Archer? She offers a possible answer when relating an incident which occurred during their bedroom scene. It was her first nude scene, and she felt rather nervous. 'When it came time . . . I took my clothes off and got into bed with Michael.' As the couple's moves progressed so did those between the Mets and the Astros, battling it out in the ninth inning on a TV set placed in the studio. 'Here I was feeling very vulnerable and sexy, and all Michael did was keep popping up in bed every two minutes to see what was happening.'

Chapter Ten

MAKING WALL STREET

October 19, 1987 – a date henceforth to be known on Wall Street as 'Black Monday'. On that fateful day, the stock market index nose-dived five hundred points – its most dramatic dip since the financial cataclysm which ushered in the Great Depression. Black Monday's long-term effects weren't half as devastating as the 'crash' of '29; nonetheless, many small investors lost everything in a single day of frenzied trading. For weeks, the entire nation awaited the outcome of the market's wildly erratic performance.

A mere eight weeks later, with our attention still focused upon the fast-paced (and incomprehensible) world of frantically bellowing floor traders and whiz kid yuppies, 20th Century-Fox unveiled their latest, timely production, *Wall Street.* Filmed entirely in Manhattan by *Platoon*'s Oscar-winning director/writer, Oliver Stone, the film starred Charlie Sheen (still 'hot' from his consecutive successes in *Lucas* and *Platoon*) as stock trader Bud Fox and Michael Douglas as corporate raider Gordon Gekko, in a dramatic saga of money and morals pulled right from contemporary headlines.

The Douglas luck struck again: As did *China Syndrome* and *Fatal Attraction*, *Wall Street* enflamed and captivated the nation's paranoid imagination, attracting flocks of press and public. And like its predecessors, *Wall Street* proved a headline maker in Michael Douglas's film career.

'I always wanted to do a business movie,' professed Oliver Stone. 'Always. My father used to take me to movies and would often say, "Why do they make the businessman such a caricature?" ' The late Lewis Stone,* himself a stockbroker, made a well-grounded critical observation: Over the years Hollywood has tended to paint the businessman's character in broad strokes, while historically cinema has contentedly overlooked Wall Street's milieu as a subject suitable to filmic treatment. Many movies have used big business as a backdrop, but few have concentrated on the dynamics and suspense inherent in trading itself.

Stock trading figures only peripherally in such films as *Marriage of a Young Stockbroker* (more about marital breakdown than stock fluctuations), *Hot Millions* (more about computer fraud), *The Bliss of Mrs Blossom* (kidnapping), *The Money Jungle* (murder), *Trading Places* (role reversal as in *The Prince and The Pauper*), or *Quicksilver* (a Horatio Alger-type tale). Likewise, television's 'Dynasty' featured sinister Dirk Maurier, an arbitrageur apparently less preoccupied with manipulating the market than manipulating the other soap characters. The general consensus seems to be that as far as motion picture entertainment goes, big business is a big bore.

Rollover, starring Jane Fonda and Kris Kristofferson, was a rare attempt (albeit unsuccessful) to engage audiences in the intricacies of international currency speculation. Like *Wall Street*, it examined the consequences of moral laxity in today's computerised business environment, where instantaneous

*To whom *Wall Street* is dedicated.

financial devastation lies at one's fingertips. However, unlike *Wall Street*, *Rollover*'s obfuscating complexities of technical lingo and plot render the movie a laborious puzzle for the viewer to decipher.

Wall Street's decisive advantage resides in the crystalline script co-written by Oliver Stone and Stanley Weiser – one doesn't need a Harvard business degree to glean the gist of what Bud Fox and Gordon Gekko are up to. Though much of the film's action dwells on boardroom and backroom wars-of-words, the central theme underlying every twist of the plot is Bud Fox's moral dilemma. Bud makes trading his life, inadvertently trading his integrity for transparent rewards of money and ego gratification.

Two father figures, Carl Fox (Martin Sheen, real life *and* movie dad*) and Gordon Gekko struggle for possession of Bud's soul, like an angel and devil perched on his shoulders. Charlie Sheen succinctly summed up Fox's moral metamorphosis: 'Bud goes through seduction, corruption and redemption.'

Fox, a young stock trader at the investment banking partnership of Jackson and Steinhem, conducts his daily business in the trading room, a hive-like environment, encompassing a wall-to-wall phalanx of desks, each crowned with telephone and desktop Quotron. At breakneck speed, cavalcades of ever-changing information recklessly tumult into the trading room, threatening to swamp the bustling traders who struggle to stay abreast of the latest developments. Teletypes and newsprinters incessantly chatter, while overhead an illuminated display flashes the latest stock index figures. Immersed in electronic din, traders violently pummel their keyboards or issue tirades,

*Martin and Charlie Sheen's only previous appearance together in a film was *The Execution of Private Slovik*. Made in 1974 for CBS, Charlie was nine years old at the time.

alternately shouting at, cajoling, or begging their wealthy clients. Atop the whole cacophony, the sales manager barks out orders, outlining the freshest stock 'menu' over p.a. speakers.

In this chaotic arena, Bud wheels and deals, a drone in a brutal business ghetto. Like a ghetto, the trading room is overcrowded, desperate, and mean. But in this ghetto, the inhabitants aren't members of an underprivileged class; rather they number amongst America's best-educated and best-paid professionals.

The bottom line in this tense, claustrophobic atmosphere is *survival*. As one character puts it, 'Every day is a blank sheet of paper.' The glory days of working one's way up through the organisation to partnership level are past; traders nowadays just concentrate on eking out a comfortable living. But Bud Fox is different; he believes he has value as an individual, he has something to contribute, and he's more than just a cog in the rich man's wheel.

His father Carl opposes Buddy's job and lifestyle; he believes in hard work and old fashioned values, and thinks his son is wasting his life and intelligence by working as a 'salesman'. Buddy agrees that he's wasting his life – he wants a shortcut to the big money. While his conceited ambition assures him that he's destined to make it, he fears the threat of burn-out which looms ever closer. Surrounded by fellow workers with failure or resignation etched on their faces, Buddy decides to break from the pack. He devises a bold plan: woo legendary corporate raider Gordon Gekko (a.k.a. 'Gekko the Great') into inviting Bud to join his team.

Gordon Gekko is notoriously reputed on 'the Street' for his underhanded business methodology. One of Buddy's fellow traders remarks that '[Gekko] was on the phone thirty seconds after the *Challenger* blew up, selling NASA stocks short*. . . . He had an ethical bypass at birth.'

Buddy obsessively pursues his well-guarded prey with daily phone calls to his private secretary. On Gekko's birthday, Bud shows up unannounced at Gekko's office, hoping to win him over with a gift of Cuban cigars and a menu of what Buddy believes are 'hot' stock recommendations. But Gekko remains unimpressed by his offerings . . . *until* Bud reluctantly dishes out an inside tip about Bluestar Airlines, the company his dad works for. Carl Fox confided to Bud that the FAA ruled a lawsuit against the airline in Bluestar's favour. When Bud exchanges this confidential information with Gekko thereby enabling him to profitably exploit the situation,** Bud takes an irrevocable step into the corrupt sphere of Gekko's influence.

The moral crisis in Bud's life is merely another scam for hundred-deals-a-day Gekko. They begin doing highly profitable business together, with Bud serving as Gordon's broker/apprentice/lackey. To fuel Bud's appetite for wealth and power, Gekko unleashes a cornucopia of temptations. At a 21 Club luncheon, he opens a million-dollar personal account with Bud. That evening, Gekko sends a gift to Bud's apartment: a prostitute in a limo who indulges him with champagne, cocaine, and backseat sex.

In exchange for these 'perks', Gekko requires some unusual business services from his broker; he has Bud spy on competitor and arch-rival, Sir Laurence Wildman (Terence Stamp). 'Sir Larry' once suckered Gekko out of a company; as recompense

*According to Stanley Weiser, Stone and he adjusted the screenplay in rewrite from present day to 1985, thereby dating it prior to the insider trading scandals that made national headlines. However, the reference to the *Challenger* tragedy, which occurred in January of '86, escaped editorial notice and was thus rendered an anachronism.

**An example of what falls into the illegal realm of 'insider trading.'

Gekko seeks a spiteful retribution for the indignity and financial loss he's suffered. Bud risks losing his licence if the SEC (Securities Exchange Commission, a watch-dog organisation) discovers he's providing Gekko with inside information. But rather than jeopardise his new-found pot of gold, Bud gives in to Gekko's demands.

Buddy's espionage enables Gekko to buy up a large quantity of stock in a steel company Wildman intends to purchase. Thwarting Wildman's plan for complete control, Gekko forces the enraged Brit to buy out his shares at a high price; Fox and he walk away from the deal reaping sizeable profits.

Increasingly enmeshed in mutual dirty dealings, Gekko bestows Bud with power of attorney to conduct business in Gordon's name (with the proviso that Gordon is off the hook if Bud gets caught), *and* with his ex-mistress, an interior designer named Darien Taylor (Darryl Hannah).

Bud advances ferociously in the business world. Soon he can easily afford a $950,000 Upper East Side apartment which Darien decorates with both her design skills and shapely body. Bud is leading the good life he's always fantasised about, but his insatiable ambition eventually overpowers his objective judgment.

Bud decides to buy Bluestar Airlines with Gekko's money and install himself as president of the company. Above his father's objections, Bud wins support from the airline unions and successfully engineers a takeover. Despite Bud's intention to turn the company around, Gekko treacherously schemes to turn it *upside down* by liquidating the hangars and planes, and scooping up $25 million from the company's employee pension fund. Gekko's plan would effectively put Bluestar out of business and put Bud's father and friends out of work.

Incensed, Bud confronts Gekko but to no avail – Gekko's not interested in anything but making as much money as he possibly can, as fast as he can. He's decided to wreck Bluestar, because it is 'wreckable'.

Fearing Fox and Gekko's inevitable showdown, Darien abandons the despairing Bud. Then, on top of all this mayhem, Bud's father suffers a heart attack. At his father's beside, Bud tearfully vows vengeance on Gekko. Retaliating the best way he knows, Bud uses the same dirty tricks Gekko taught him to manoeuvre Bluestar out of Gekko's grasp and into the hands of his nemesis, Sir Laurence Wildman.

Although he's managed to save Bluestar and vindicate himself in his father's eyes, Bud's past catches up with him, and he gets to relish his triumphant coup all too briefly. Humiliated before all his constituents at Jackson and Steinhem, Bud is arrested by the SEC and led away handcuffed.

As a parting shot against his treacherous boss, Bud goes to meet Gekko with a 'bug' planted on him, planning to entrap him in a confession. Gekko beats and kicks Buddy, but unwittingly indicts himself by revealing too much in the course of his enraged rebuke. The movie ends on a note of salvation: en route to his trial, Bud admits that he sold himself for hollow dreams and shallow pleasures, and realises that he must begin his life anew.

The unmitigated greed for money and thirst for power that *Wall Street*'s characters exhibit is no exaggeration. Kenneth Lipper, Stone's chief technical adviser for *Wall Street* and author of its novelisation, bore personal witness to the devastating blindness that besets men on both ends of the balance of power. Lipper, a former partner at the venerable investment banking firm of Lehman Brothers,* saw his former company gradually rent asunder as its two top executive officers battled for position at the helm. As detailed in the book, *Greed and Glory on Wall*

*Revered as one of Wall St's oldest continuing partnerships.

Street, the fall of the house of Lehman was brought about not exclusively by a change of fortune, but by obstinate and egotistically motivated mismanagement. Formerly Wall Street's billion-dollar powerhouse, the company ended up on the auction block after debilitating years of internal intrigue, deceit, and cowardice.

Dirty tricks are a sordid fact of life on 'the Street'; whether revealed in the pages of respected publications like *Fortune* or *The Wall Street Journal*, or overheard on the grapevine, gossip concerning the financial activities of the 'men-who-make-the-money-roll' can set a company's stock prices off on a roller coaster ride. This is the kind of underhanded influence Gekko exerts when instructing Bud to leak rumours about a company's financial status to his fellow traders or send coded messages to a journalist ally at a financial paper.

Gekko's 'tricks' have historical precedent: in 1984, scandal hit *The Wall Street Journal* when R. Foster Winans, contributing writer to its 'Heard On The Street' column (an innuendo-laden hodge-podge of investment tips, spot analysis, and economic speculation), confessed leaking items from upcoming columns to select traders. The traders would then divide the profits between themselves, Winans and his boyfriend. The SEC charged that Winans's tips led to 46 cases of insider trading in the stock of twenty-seven companies, and involved two of Kidder Peabody's high-ranking salesmen.

In the real world, tactics can sometimes get as downright personal as Gekko's tiff with Sir Larry. Michael Cieply, another former *Journal* reporter, recalled that an investment banker once hinted that he could provide him with an abundance of inside tips and sources if Cieply helped him 'get something' on a fellow reporter who was making life tough for his firm. Hoping to fuel rumours, the banker inquired, 'Does he like boys?'

Cieply also remembered that the one time he actually

received a coded tip from a banker, his editor derisively scoffed, 'Now how on earth do you figure we could use a cock-eyed thing like that?'

Falling hot on the heels of *Fatal Attraction*, *Wall Street* solidly established Michael Douglas as a major box-office draw. All of a sudden he found that 'my acting life has totally changed. I'm the flavour of the month.' Until *Wall Street*, the brass ring of recognition had eluded him.

Never fully appreciated as an actor, Douglas wondered for most of his career when he would finally win widespread critical acknowledgment of his talent. Michael Douglas reported in *Parade* magazine a conversation he'd once conducted with his father: 'I asked, "Dad, when was the first time you had a role that you said to yourself, 'This is my role, I'm making it my part,' and you can't think of anyone who could do it better? You have such a sense . . . of just eating this part up?" He said, "*Champion*". That was where he initiated this incredible persona, this fierceness, this killer quality that overrode everything, this tremendous intensity, this anger, this strength, this erupting volcano.'

It was the same darkly molten intensity that Michael unearthed from himself when he enveloped himself in the ruthlessly belligerent character of Gordon Gekko.

Webster's Dictionary defines the gecko as a big-headed, weak-limbed lizard that preys on small insects. Geckos have pads on the bottoms of their toes, covered with minute hooks; these enable the reptile to swiftly and agilely scuttle up vertical surfaces and even walk upside down.

The metaphor is obvious, but appropriate: Mr Gordon Gekko, with a hungry animal's cold-blooded disregard for moral propriety, is a man who's slithered up social and economic ladders to a remote level, seemingly as unapproachable as the elusive gecko clinging atop a ceiling.

This role was by no means consistent with the type of parts Michael had taken on in the past. Although they were all aggressive in their own way – the peevish shutterbug of *The China Syndrome*, the abrasive director of *A Chorus Line*, the roguish smart alec of *Romancing the Stone* and *Jewel of the Nile* – none of these characters radiated Gordon Gekko's negative magnitude, his vengeful, unscrupulous solipsism. 'I loved playing somebody off the nose,' Douglas says of Gekko, 'somebody who is so self-absorbed and self-involved that what believes to be true – that it's a dog-eat-dog world and the ends justify the means – is what everybody else in the world must believe also.'

Anxious to establish his own reputation and avoid critical comparisons with his old man, Michael often played polar opposite types to Kirk Douglas's prototypic, jutting-jawed, uncompromising man of action. Michael instead cultivated his own on-screen persona – the sardonic but sensitive man of *reaction* – and elaborated on this figure throughout the bulk of his oeuvres.

Although Michael generally denies any hint of rivalry or competition between himself and his father, he acknowledges that 'as a child you think, "How can I be the man my father is?" It takes a long time to get through all of that to a sense of yourself.'

Eager to prove himself as more than just junior dimple-chin, Michael selected roles unbefitting the classic Kirk Douglas model. The result was as Michael had hoped: comparisons between the two actors' styles often short-circuited under analysis. However, Michael eventually realised that his self-imposed dramaturgical diet contained a double-edged blade. By strictly confining himself to the world of anti-Kirk roles, Michael found himself giving up some choice parts, and therefore unable to fully explore his potential range as an actor. He discovered that such arbitrary selectiveness 'limits you a little' and self-consciousness while performing can inhibit or alter an actor's interpretation of a part.

All along Kirk assured Michael that when he finally took up the challenge of playing a bad guy, he was going to completely surprise all the cynics who thought Michael could only handle bland nice-guy routines. Perhaps Kirk knew, both from his own painful enmity towards his father, and his hard-earned reputation in the vicious world of showbiz, that Michael stored a veritable warehouse of potential hostility beneath his easy-going exterior. Michael told *Rolling Stone*, 'My father has always said, "You're going to do a great killer sometime. You're such a charming guy, but they're gonna find out the prick you really are." '

When Michael finally played the big heavy, all his vengeful energy erupted. It was apparent that Michael not only pulled it off with aplomb, but he'd come into his own as an actor.

For Michael, the ultimate accolade for his *Wall Street* performance came not from the mouths of critics; it was the rave review he received from his dad that impressed him the most. 'My father paid me the greatest compliment,' Michael beamed. 'He said, "Son I noticed the resemblance between us but, five minutes into the picture I forgot you were my son, I forgot everything. You really nailed that part!" '

When he slid into Gordon Gekko's slimy lizard suit, Michael advanced onto an untested limb. Shifting gears from *Fatal Attraction*'s stupefied victim to *Wall Street*'s manipulative Mephistopheles, Michael had to adjust his mental attitude from its usual mellow groove to full frontal assault. For him it proved no easy turnaround. 'It was hard holding that clean cutting edge,' he told *People* magazine.

What initially attracted Oliver Stone to Michael Douglas

was his performance in *Romancing the Stone*. Oliver says he saw 'an edge to [Douglas] which I found interesting.' Although they'd met only twice casually, Stone knew that, as a producer, Michael had a good deal of hands-on experience in the business world; this experience, Stone believed, was crucial to accurately moulding Gekko's character. Casting Douglas as a big-time financier 'wasn't really casting against type,' Stone assured *Rolling Stone* magazine. 'He lives in that world.'

Indeed, Michael's sometimes frustrating experiences trying to raise capital for his projects provided him with ample opportunities to rub elbows with investment bankers and their ilk. His business experience offered real men to model Gekko on, but also contributed to his motivation: 'The other thing I drew from my produciary background is that *revenge is wonderful*. Gekko thrives on the energy of anybody who's ever crossed him. He cherishes holding grudges. It gives him the fuel to keep going. I know that during all the years when I dealt with rejection on film projects, it was an emotion that, directed in a positive way, gave me the endurance and stamina that I needed to get a picture made. Or in Gordon's case, to get deals done.'

Michael also fleshed out his research conducting a personal interview with Asher Edelman, and intensively studying television footage of some major corporate titans of the moment. One such subject was Carl Icahn, New York financier and practitioner of the subversive business strategy known as 'greenmail'.

A greenmailer buys up enough shares of a target company's stock to effect a takeover; if the company's other shareholders resist the takeover attempt they're compelled to purchase the greenmailer's stock at premium prices. Mr Icahn's organisation walked off with a $30 million profit from one such 'deal'.

Michael paid close attention to T. Boone Pickens Jr., wily Texas oilman and possibly the most feared corporate raider on the American business scene. From 1984 through '85, his flagship company of Mesa Petroleum reshaped the American oil industry by buying into and then selling out of companies like Phillips Petroleum (to the tune of $89 million) and Gulf Oil (earning Pickens' backers $760 million when he sold his stock to Standard Oil).

The man generally considered to be the closest real-life model for Gekko is Ivan F. Boesky, arbitrageur and billionaire investor. Boesky, arrested back in 1986 on federal charges of illegal insider trading, is forever banned from trading in the US securities industry. Back when he was still an active player in the takeover game, Mr Boesky delivered a commencement speech which served as basis and inspiration for the infamous 'Greed is good' speech Douglas utters midway through the movie.

Gekko's avaricious sermon is delivered at an annual shareholders' meeting for a company he intends to take over. Deriding the company's large board of directors for wasteful mismanagement, and heralding himself as a crusader dedicated to revitalising dying, bloated companies, he rallies the other stockholders to his side. Climaxing with a litany of greed's beneficial contributions to mankind's progress, Gekko concludes that greed is a higher truth, containing the antidote to all business woes, and the ultimate salvation of the United States.

The first time Douglas completed the nine-minute monologue in a single take, the six hundred extras in attendance applauded uproariously. Although they'd been instructed to applaud, Douglas was beginning to feel his oats: 'I believed I was taking over a company.' This sequence and Douglas's locker room scolding of Fox are generally regarded as stand-out clips, and possibly Douglas's finest moments in the movie.

The fetishistic array of accessories Gekko adorns himself with 'was the key' to his psyche, claimed Douglas. 'Things like cufflinks, braces, immediately gave me a costume. [Gekko's] idea of being really well-dressed is probably a little flashy.' But this 'flashiness' provides Gekko, as it does a gaudy street pimp, with a conspicuous emblem of power.

Wall Street's costume designer, Ellen Mirojnick, arranged direct consultation for Michael with the man who dresses real-life Wall Street tycoons, Alan Flusser. A Coty-award-winning designer, Flusser embodies the look of the impeccably well-groomed and well-to-do. From their first meeting at Douglas's apartment, the contrast between the two men was painfully apparent. Flusser showed up wearing 'pretty much what I always do' – a double-breasted suit with cuffs on the jacket sleeves, wing-tip suede shoes, and a horizontal stripe shirt with a white collar. Douglas, on the other hand, was a trifle more casually attired in dark pants and a white broadcloth shirt.

Although hardly mirror images, Douglas and Flusser at least shared common aesthetic ground as far as Flusser's Sylvester and Tweety Bird braces were concerned; Michael admired them so much he wanted to purchase an extra pair for Jack Nicholson. But after three weeks of sifting through Flusser's midtown menswear boutique, Michael epitomised the very image of expensive elegance. According to *People* magazine, Douglas's pricey duds (now residing in his closet) included eleven suits [$975 to $1,500 each and tailored from English and Italian worsteds), twenty-four Swiss and English cotton shirts (at $250 a shot), and an assortment of handsewn silk ties. The $28,000 spent on Douglas's film wardrobe was about seventeen per cent of the movie's total wardrobe budget, but by Mirojnick's account it was a wise investment because 'Michael comes across as someone incredibly strong and awesome.'

Flusser bolstered the impression by subtly exaggerating the dimensions of Douglas's five-foot-ten, hundred-and-fifty-pound frame. By widening the cuffs, inserting shoulder pads, and tapering the collar points to sharp forty-five degree angles, Flusser lent the unthreatening-looking Douglas, in his own words, 'more powerful proportions'. The ubiquitous braces weren't there only for looks. According to Flusser, 'Douglas is very thin through the hips; if he hadn't worn braces, I doubt his pants would've stayed up.' Michael's frame might not be ideally proportioned, but Flusser does say, Michael 'could probably wear anything and pull it off.'

(After the movie came out, sales at Flusser's boutique more than doubled from customers in search of the 'power look', and Flusser modestly projected earnings of $2 million by the year's end.)

Examining Icahn, Pickens, and Boesky, Douglas sought out overall similarities while homing in on idiosyncratic mannerisms, and slowly pieced together his Frankenstein. He explained his *modus operandi* to the *New York Times*: 'You take essences. In some you pick up on the intellect. In some the killer instinct – you can see it in the eyes. I never saw Gekko as a bully – he didn't need to be. The ones I know in really powerful positions can afford to be humble.'

Gordon Gekko first came into Michael Douglas's life in the form of a sixty-page sheaf of script. Though it entailed a salary cut from his *Fatal Attraction* earnings, advance word on *Wall Street* was lively, and Michael wanted the part. Nevertheless studio executives opposed Stone's choice; they considered Michael too young for the part.* 'Somebody told Oliver when he hired me, "Ah, he's going to be off working on five different things," ' reported Douglas. Michael's production company did have sixteen different scripts in development while he was making *Wall Street*, but Michael put blinders on. 'I was spreading

*Carl Icahn, for example, hit fifty-three in 1988.

myself thin,' he said of his preoccupation with producing. 'I discovered again the real joy of acting which had been missing.'

Not since his university days had Michael approached an acting job with such trepidation. The problem confronting him largely centred around technique: in a role that consisted of standing, sitting, or pacing about, eulogising about money, Michael had to devise a way to keep his lengthy monologues from sounding monotonous or speechy.

Arriving on the set with a preconceived notion of how the script went, Michael's occasional difficulty in remembering lines was further hindered by last-minute changes; key details such as company names hinged on the director's whims. 'You've got this whole long rhythm of these speeches,' Douglas observed, 'just throwing these names off the tip of your tongue, and now in the back of your mind, all you're thinking of is trying to remember the name change.'

From day one, Michael struggled to impart the right feel to Gekko's pontifications but sometimes he found his interpretations at odds with Mr Stone's wishes. Once when Michael offered to reshoot a scene to Stone's satisfaction, Stone adamantly declined, saying, 'John Ford never reshot.' Later, Michael screened the scene in question at the dailies, liked what he saw and confronted Stone about his performance. 'This is pretty good,' Michael challenged. Stone replied, 'It is, isn't it?' 'You fucker,' Michael grumbled.

Stone's open criticism was by no means personal; the entire cast was treated to liberal pepperings of critique. Charlie Sheen found Stone's behaviour comparatively consistent with the way he'd directed *Platoon*; he characterised Stone as 'brutally honest. Which is why we clicked. After a scene he'd say, "You sucked", or "You nailed it". That's just my style.'

In retrospect, Michael saw Oliver's frankness as a way of toughening him up to play the callous, hard nut he portrayed.

While Oliver Stone may not be a warmly demonstrative director, and his confrontational style may put friend and foe alike on the spot, he's nonetheless earned the respect of his peers. Michael believes that Stone, though not outwardly supportive, backed him a hundred per cent. 'I always reminded myself, "Hey, he offered you this part. This is a great part." ' Charlie Sheen declares that, 'After my dad, Oliver's the man with the most integrity of anybody I've ever known. And he's a brilliant film maker.'

As movie-makers, Douglas and Stone have more in common than might first spring to mind. Michael doesn't wear his political/ethical conscience on his sleeve, but he's always been attracted to issue-oriented films, from the time of *Hail Hero!* to present day projects. Stone earned kudos for *Salvador*, but two years prior, Michael co-produced a televised debate about the embattled country.

A member of the Committee of Concern for Central America, Michael gathered eight representatives of right, left and centre factions for a diplomatic broadcast presented by Los Angeles's KCET. About a quarter of a million viewers tuned in to watch the programme entitled 'El Salvador: The Road to Peace.'

During filming, Stone and Douglas often jokingly sparred over politics. Michael told *Rolling Stone*, 'He teases me about my not getting my fingers dirty any more – being a producer and financing my films on Wall Street. I tease him that his career *did* exist before *Salvador*. I like to remind him of *The Hand*.'*

Michael and Oliver weren't the only sparring partners to be found on the set of *Wall Street*; Charlie Sheen and actress Sean Young, who plays Mrs Kate Gekko, locked horns while working

*An absolutely abysmal re-make of *The Beast With Five Fingers*.

together, until they reached the point where they barely communicated. Charlie gloated to the *Daily News* that one day after 'she really pissed me off, I took this napkin and I wrote [a four-letter word describing a part of the female anatomy] on it and put it on her back while she wasn't looking. She walked around like that for a while. People loved it. The next day we had a big fight about it.' Charlie made it clear he relished the notion of never dealing with Ms Young again. 'I feel sorry for her because she has to wake up with herself every day,' he said.*

Personality conflicts among the cast trifled next to the bidding war that raged between *Forbes* and *Fortune* over placing their magazines in *Wall Street* as props. In the scene where Charlie first appears in Gekko's office, he's toting a copy of a financial mag which he cites as 'the Bible'. Both *Forbes* and *Fortune* desired to be the beneficiary of this accolade.

In the original script, Stone slated *Fortune* as the magazine he'd used, but 20th Century-Fox, scenting a potential cash-in, sent copies of the script to both magazines. *Fortune* opened with an offer of a free page of advertising, worth over $47,000 as its bid for stardom. *Forbes* countered with two pages of free advertising, worth more than $92,000. Matching the number of pages *Forbes* offered, *Fortune* upped the ante to $94,208, and pointed out that *Fortune* often uses individuals on their covers, while *Forbes* does so rarely – and they sent over their six latest issues to prove it.

'There was a stage where there was some frantic pitching going on,' noted Gary Belis, a spokesman for *Fortune*. 'I pointed out that if they were trying to establish the Charlie Sheen character as a kid on the make, the word "fortune" means a lot of money. *Forbes* has no meaning as a word.'

*Certain members of the press implied that due to Sean Young's on set behaviour, her role had to be pared down.

When Stone decided to go with *Fortune*, as he'd originally planned, the magazine tried to capitalise on their victory by proposing a cover picturing Fox, post-arrest, with the headline 'Yuppie With a Conscience'. By Belis's account Stone went for the idea and shot a scene with Carl Fox reading the issue, but in the final cut Fox's cover was omitted, and the Gekko cover is only fleetingly visible. Stone noted in *Playboy* that he used both magazines as props anyway.

One publication that definitely *didn't* want to be included was *The Wall Street Journal*. Stone complained, '*The Wall Street Journal* had a strange attitude towards the movie. We asked to use the paper as a prop, but they turned us down. We also asked about shooting in their offices and they turned us down for that. I'm not surprised; they are very conservative and they're nervous. There's a scene in the movie where a journalist gets an inside tip and uses that information to get what he needs for his story.'

As expected, *Wall Street* raised the ire of a lot of people in and out of the business community. Irwin Jacobs, rated by *Fortune* as one of the country's biggest corporate raiders, denounced the film: 'The sad thing is, a lot of people are going to see this and believe this is the way Wall Street is run.' Jacobs considered the film little more than a flimsy disguised portrait of Ivan Boesky whom he described as a 'pathetic' figure. 'This is not a form of business, this is a form of sickness,' he said of the stock market shenanigans depicted in the movie. 'You don't have to do it that way.'

Jacobs also claimed that Stone had distorted the role corporate raiders serve in restructuring corporations and the economy. 'It isn't like these people went and robbed banks or put guns to anybody's head,' he protested. 'These people served a purpose. This small group shook up a lot of people.'

Would Jacobs be surprised to find Stone echoing this viewpoint? 'Some of these guys are sharks,' said Stone. 'They're killers, but I think a lot of what the raiders do is good. Lots of companies in this country really stink – the auto business, the steel industry – with their bloated, fat-cat management. I admire men like T. Boone Pickens and Carl Icahn, who can shake up the entrenched mentality. In that sense these guys are like pirates and buccaneers.'

Controversy over moral questions raised by the movie ricocheted from magazine to paper, with critics and editorialists either agreeing wholeheartedly with Stone or lambasting him for oversimplifying the issues. George Will warned in the *Daily News* of *Wall Street*'s 'yuppie populism' and described it as a 'morality soap opera' that 'spouts statistical rubbish'. New York City's Mayor Edward Koch criticised the ending for taking 'a turn for the simplistic'. *People* magazine film reviewer Scot Haller charged, 'Stone lectures like a dull preacher. It's as if nobody ever threw the money changers out of the temple and he has just discovered the sin of greed.'

While critics complained of *Wall Street*'s ineffectiveness, the movie's impact snowballed. *Newsweek*'s January 4 cover announced, 'The '80s Are Over: Greed Goes Out of Style'. The *New York Times*, in successive editions, featured articles reflecting on 'greed', not only in its review of *Wall Street*, but on the front page of the Arts and Leisure section, in a business section report, on the Op Ed page, and in an editorial. For a tiresome oversimplification, *Wall Street* seemed to generate copious amounts of wide-ranging debate and coverage.

As regards Michael Douglas's performance, the acclaim was almost universally voiced. Even critics who panned the film singled Douglas out for enthusiastic approval. 'When Michael Douglas is terrorising the town in Oliver Stone's funny-money melodrama, he's the scariest monster since Faye Dunaway cleaned house in *Mommie Dearest*. . . . Douglas is Satan in a high-priced suit and he gives the kind of razzle-dazzle performance that defines a career.' (*People* magazine) Kathleen Carroll of the *Daily News* said, 'It's a kick to watch Douglas tear up the scenery with such bullish intensity . . . Michael Douglas plays Gekko to the hilt.' *New York* magazine praised Michael's performance as 'charismatic, irresistible' and commended Stone for portraying 'the lure of big money so vivid you can savour it like Stilton and port.'

Perhaps the final word on *Wall Street*'s impact comes from Mel Brooks, who reported in *Premiere* magazine that his upcoming comedy was called *Money, Money, Money*, starring Brooks as a 'bloodsucking stockbroker' and Rick Moranis as a green Harvard Business School grad. Brooks announced that he would 'probably make fun of' *Wall Street*, but he still hadn't seen it. However, he did note reassuringly that 'I have to see it right away.'

Chapter Eleven

OSCAR EPILOGUE

'It's all gravy now.'

– Michael Douglas, after his Oscar nomination.

'Yeah, I've got them all out working. The only one who's still doing nothing is my grandson Cameron [then three]. I don't understand it. He seems to think he can get away with it just because he's got a dimple on his chin like mine . . .'

– Kirk Douglas, '82

'I think very often I was harder on Michael and Joel, because I was spending split time with them. One of the ways a father can show he cares is by bawling the hell out of them. I thought, well, maybe one day they'll remember I wasn't indifferent to them. . . . I wasn't there with a whip, but I think I have a much warmer relationship with my kids now than I did then.'

– Kirk Douglas, '88

To Kirk Douglas, it may have seemed like Hollywood did it on purpose. From the beginning of his movie career through its first decade, the Academy took notice of him every three or four years, held out the little gold statue, and yanked it away. First there came *Champion*, possibly an understandable oversight because of the anti-hero nature of the character he played and the fact that it was his first nomination. Then, in 1952, *The Bad and the Beautiful*. The performance, as well as the entire movie, is a tribute to the considerable talents of those involved. It won five Oscars out of six: Best Supporting Actress, Costumes, Cinematography, Screenplay, Art Direction/Set Decor . . . but once again, Kirk found himself left behind. Perhaps the somewhat sensitive area he probed in his portrayal of a ruthless film executive had an influence on the voters' decisions, but it's hard to imagine when watching the movie today.

Douglas's nomination for his startling and moving performance as Vincent Van Gogh in *Lust For Life* brought the biggest disappointment of all several years later. He loved the part, he loved the movie perhaps more than any other movie he's done besides *Lonely Are the Brave*. People thought he had it sewn up, but it went to Gary Cooper for *High Noon*. Since that 1956 role, Kirk Douglas has received plenty of awards, but no more Oscar nominations.

In 1984, Kirk wouldn't come straight out and vent his spleen at the Academy. 'Yes, I would like to win an Oscar because it is an award given by your peers. . . . All in all, the Oscars have been more fair than most other awards, except how they could not give it to me was a bit of stupidity.'

In 1973, he managed to be a tad more whimsical. 'Wouldn't it be great to do a picture of the loser's acceptance speeches?' he asked a reporter.

Besides, he won Academy accolades indirectly in 1976, when *One Flew Over the Cuckoo's Nest* swept up every important award. Besides Best Picture, the property Kirk had handed over to Michael to produce made a memorable showing. Jack Nicholson won Best Actor, Milos Forman won Best Director, Louise Fletcher thanked her deaf parents in sign language when she picked up her Best Actress Award, and Lawrence Hauben and Bo Goldman won for Best Screenplay. Michael Douglas was launched into the movie business with a vengeance, and he and Kirk were somewhat vindicated for the problems they suffered trying to bring the movie to the screen.

The Douglas Clan and the Oscars didn't meet again in a significant way until 1988, when Michael Douglas received the Best Actor nomination for his role in *Wall Street*. He also racked up the opposite of 'Guilt By Association' kudos for his involvement in the heavily nominated *Fatal Attraction*, which popped up in the Best Actress, Best Supporting Actress, Best Picture, Best Director, Best Editing, and Best Screenplay Adaptation categories. Wherever one looked, Michael Douglas's name appeared in conjunction with the Academy Awards. Critic after critic named him as most likely to succeed for his dynamic portrayal of everybody's favourite pin-up corporate raider, Gordon Gekko. Otherwise, *Wall Street*, unlike its predecessor *Platoon*, was virtually ignored.

Several months earlier, the *New York Times* carried an article covering a tribute staged at Kirk's alma mater, the AADA, which featured the presence of all four of his scattered sons. In the course of the interview, reporter Leslie Bennetts enquired as to Kirk's disposition and feelings in conjunction with Michael's ever-growing success. The proud father replied that his son's success made him feel immortal. 'It's narcissistic. But narcissism is a nice word. Self-love is important. Maturity means falling in love with yourself, in the sense of understanding yourself and saying, "Hey – I'm not such a bad guy." You change, and you have to come to grips with yourself – and make peace with yourself. I think the most elegant form of narcissism is your children.'

At the tribute, which followed closely on the heels of a Lifetime Achievement Award, Michael announced: 'My father always wanted to be an actor, and it's amazing to see all the roles he's played. He's played a soldier, a painter, a Viking, architect, boxer, and many others . . . but of all the roles he's played, I want to congratulate him publicly on his role as father.'

The big nomination also brought a lot of unwelcome attention from the tabloids; speculation as to the state of Michael and Diandra's marriage almost obliterated speculation as to who would win what. Michael steadfastly denied everything and tried to keep his chin up as D-Day approached.

One week the *Enquirer* featured a front-page story of the Douglases' 'bizarre' marriage, citing in the role of other woman Sabrina Guinness, the British heiress who had dated Prince Charles, Mick Jagger, and Jack Nicholson. The tale of marital strife and woe painted a rather sorry picture of Diandra, who according to an 'inside source' rejected the idea of divorce because 'she enjoys being Mrs Michael Douglas. Married to a hot actor . . . Diandra knows that most of her entrée to the most exclusive parties and social events is because of the glitter and power of her husband.' This came soon after the widely quoted *W* magazine list of what's 'In' and what's 'Out' split the couple by putting Michael on the 'In' list and sticking Diandra on the 'Out' list.

Shortly after the *Enquirer* article, the *Star* ran another front-page story, crediting Kirk with helping to mend a few fences between the two, who were shown walking happily down the beach with Cameron in tow. All in all, this increased exposure of his private affairs couldn't have made the wait between nomination and the Oscar ceremony any easier for the Douglases.

On the evening of April 11, Michael and Diandra made a

grand entrance, dressed smartly, he in formal, she in a provocative black number. After sitting through the usual questionable musical acts and endless jokes about the writers' strike, Michael finally came forward to accept his award. With the crowd's noisy verbal approval still echoing in the hall, he looked at the statue and launched into his acceptance speech for 'a role that not many people thought I could play.'

'I'd like to dedicate this award to my parents and step-parents, who have been supportive over the years, and particularly to my father, who I don't think ever missed one of my college productions, for his continued support, and in particular for helping his son step out of his shadow. I'll be eternally grateful to you, Dad.' He also thanked Diandra, who was shown crying her eyes out in the audience, and said good night to Cameron, while holding the Oscar aloft. Altogther a moving moment in Oscar history, and one the Douglas Clan will always treasure.

Later, backstage, the press enquired as to the whereabouts of Kirk. As it turned out, Father watched at home. 'He was too nervous to come,' Michael explained, noting the time when Dad had been assured of the Oscar and lost. He continued, 'My father carved a very strong image early in his career, and it took me a while to carve out a niche for myself. I've talked to people like Charlie Sheen about the same problem.' When asked how it felt to have an Oscar when his father didn't, Michael said, 'Well, he was nominated three times and by the luck of the draw never selected – and luck is really what it is. I hope I was clear that I share this with him.'

Michael and Diandra toted the shiny statuette off to a party at Kirk and Anne's house to share it as soon as possible. The fête at the senior Douglas's Beverly Hills home was only one of many they attended that night, though certainly the most important (with no offence to Swifty Lazar). They also showed up at a glittering but somewhat quiet and private celebration at an exclusive club called Helena's, where Michael livened things up by bringing an entourage of at least twenty well-wishers. And lest you forget, the whole long evening began with a fabulous pre-awards party at the home of VIP Dawn Steel, who hosted two hundred celebrities at a buffet supper, which some expectant nominees, like Michael, were probably too nervous to eat. At least the company was good. Guests included Gregory Peck, Danny DeVito, Billy Crystal, Stanley Jaffe, Glenn Close, Anne Archer, and Sherry Lansing.

After the post-Awards brouhaha, Michael and Diandra headed back to home base supposedly to begin sorting out their difficulties. As rumours continued to circulate, friends expressed public sympathy and good wishes for the couple, citing the recent strain of a miscarriage they suffered through several months previously as a factor contributing to their problems, although at the time the couple managed to keep their grief private. Such speculation added a note of tragedy to Michael's triumph.

Michael Douglas referred to the possibility of his winning as 'the cherry on the top,' a modest reference perhaps, unless you think of it as a cherry the size of King Kong sitting on top of a career as impressive as the Empire State Building. One thing is for sure, Michael will continue to do his family name proud, and the Douglases will go down in history as one of Hollywood's most impressive, 'functioning' family units.

FILMOGRAPHY

'A performer should be judged on a body of work, not a single picture, or even two or three.'

– Kirk Douglas '70

Lonely Are the Brave (1962)
Produced by: Edward Lewis
Directed by: David Miller
Cast: Kirk Douglas, Gena Rowlands, Walter Matthau, Michael Kane, Carrol O'Connor, George Kennedy, William Schallert, Karl Swenson
Screenplay by: Dalton Trumbo. Based on Edward Abbey's novel *Brave Cowboy*
(Michael Douglas worked as a gofer/part-time editor on this production.)
107 minutes; A Joel Production (Kirk Douglas)
Distributed by: Universal-International

The Heroes of Telemark (1965, British)
Produced by: S. Benjamin Fisz
Directed by: Anthony Mann
Cast: Kirk Douglas, Richard Harris, Ulla Jacobsen, Michael

Redgrave, David Weston, Eric Porter, Anton Diffring, Mervyn Johns
Screenplay by Ivan Moffat and Ben Barzman, based on *But For These Men* by John Drummond and Knut Haukelid's *Skis Against The Atom*
Assistant Director: Michael Douglas
131 minutes; A Benton Film Production
Distributed by: Columbia (USA) and Rank (UK)

Cast a Giant Shadow (1966)
Produced by: Mel Shavelson
Directed by: Mel Shavelson
Cast: Kirk Douglas, Yul Brynner, John Wayne, Senta Berger, Angie Dickinson, James Donald, Frank Sinatra, Luther Adler, Topol
Screenplay by: Mel Shavelson, based on the book by Ted Berkman
Production Assistant: Michael Douglas
142 minutes; A Mirisch-Lienroe–Batjac Production
Distributed by: United Artists

Hail, Hero! (1969)
Produced by: Harold D. Cohen
Directed by: David Miller
Cast: Michael Douglas, Arthur Kennedy, Teresa Wright, John Larch, Charles Drake, Peter Strauss
Screenplay based on a novel by John Weston
Originally 100 minutes, cut to 97 minutes; A Cinema Center Film/Halcyon Production
Distributed by: National General

Adam At 6 AM (1970)
Produced by: A Cinema Center Film

Directed by: Robert Scheerer
Cast: Michael Douglas, Lee Purcell, Joe Don Baker, Grayson Hall, Charles Aidman, Meg Foster
Screenplay by: Stephen and Elinor Karpf
100 minutes; A Cinema Center Films Production

Summertree (1971)
Produced by: Kirk Douglas
Directed by: Anthony Newley
Cast: Michael Douglas, Jack Warden, Brenda Vaccaro, Barbara Bel Geddes, Bill Vint, Kirk Callaway
Screenplay based on the off-Broadway play by Ron Cowen
88 minutes; A Bryna Production
Distributed by: Columbia Pictures

When Michael Calls (1971, a made-for-television movie)
Produced by: Gil Shiva
Directed by: Philip Leacock
Cast: Ben Gazzara, Elizabeth Ashley, Michael Douglas, Karen Pearson, Albert S. Waxman
Screenplay by: James Bridges, based on a novel by John Farris
73 minutes; A Palomar Pictures International Production
Distributed by: 20th Century-Fox

Napoleon and Samantha (1972)
Produced by: Walt Disney Productions
Directed by: Bernard McEveety
Cast: Michael Douglas, Jodie Foster, Johnny Whitaker, Will Greer, Henry Jones, Arch Johnson, Ellen Corby
Screenplay by: Stewart Raffill
92 minutes
Video distributed by: Walt Disney Home Video

The Streets of San Francisco (1972, a made-for-television movie/pilot for the series)
Produced by: Quinn Martin
Cast: Karl Malden, Michael Douglas, Robert Wagner, Kim Darby, Andrew Duggan, John Rubinstein, Tom Bosley, Edward Andrews, Mako
Screenplay by: Ed Hume, based on Carolyn Weston's *Poor, Poor Ophelia*
98 minutes; A Quinn Martin Production

One Flew Over the Cuckoo's Nest (1976)
Produced by: Michael Douglas and Saul Zaentz
Directed by: Milos Forman
Cast: Jack Nicholson, Louise Fletcher, Brad Dourif, William Redfield, Michael Berryman, Peter Brocco, Will Sampson, Danny DeVito, Christopher Lloyd, Scatman Crothers, Vincent Schiavelli, Louisa Moritz
Screenplay by: Lawrence Hauben and Bo Goldman, based on the novel by Ken Kesey
133 minutes
Video distributed by: HBO Home Video

Coma (1978)
Produced by: Martin Erlichman
Directed by: Michael Crichton
Cast: Genevieve Bujold, Michael Douglas, Rip Torn, Elizabeth Ashley, Richard Widmark, Lance LeGault, Lois Chiles, Tom Selleck
Screenplay by: Michael Crichton, based on Robin Cook's novel
113 minutes
Video distributed by: MGM/UA Home Video

The China Syndrome (1979)
Produced by: Michael Douglas
Directed by: James Bridges
Cast: Jane Fonda, Jack Lemmon, Michael Douglas, James Hampton, Scott Brady, Peter Donat, Wilford Brimley, James Karen, Diandra Morrell (Douglas)
Screenplay by: Mike Gray and T. S. Cook and James Bridges
123 minutes; A Michael Douglas/IPC Films Presentation
Distributed by: Columbia Pictures
Video distributed by: Columbia Pictures Home Video

Running (1979, Canadian)
Produced by: Robert Cooper and Ronald Cohen
Directed by: Steven Hilliard Stern
Cast: Michael Douglas, Susan Anspach, Lawrence Dane, Eugene Levy, Charles Shamata, Philip Akin
Screenplay by: Steven Hilliard Stern
103 minutes; A Universal Picture

It's My Turn (1980)
Produced by: Martin Elfand
Directed by: Claudia Weill
Cast: Jill Clayburgh, Michael Douglas, Charles Grodin, Beverly Garland, Teresa Baxter, Steven Hill, Joan Copeland, John Gabriel
Screenplay by: Eleanor Bergstein
91 minutes; A Columbia Picture
Video distributed by: Film Fair Communications

The Star Chamber (1983)
Produced by: Frank Yablans
Directed by: Peter Hyams
Cast: Michael Douglas, Hal Holbrook, Yaphet Kotto,

Sharon Gless, James B. Sikking, Joe Regalbuto, Don Calfa, DeWayne Jessie, Jack Kehoe, Diana Dill, Douglas Darrid
Screenplay by: Roderick Taylor and Peter Hyams
109 minutes; A 20th Century-Fox Picture
Video distributed by: CBS/Fox Video

Romancing the Stone (1984)
Produced by: Michael Douglas
Directed by: Robert Zemeckis
Cast: Michael Douglas, Kathleen Turner, Danny DeVito, Zack Norman, Alfonso Arau, Manuel Ojeda, Holland Taylor
Screenplay by: Diane Renee Thomas
105 minutes
Distributed by: 20th Century-Fox
Video distributed by: CBS/Fox Video

Starman (1984)
Produced by: Michael Douglas
Directed by: John Carpenter
Cast: Jeff Bridges, Karen Allen, Charles Martin Smith, Richard Jaeckel
Screenplay by: Bruce Evans and Raynold Gideon
115 minutes; A Columbia Picture

A Chorus Line (1985)
Produced by: Cy Feuer and Ernest Martin
Directed by: Richard Attenborough
Cast: Michael Douglas, Terrence Mann, Alyson Reed, Cameron English, Vicki Frederick, Audrey Landers, Nicole Fosse, Greg Burge, Janet Jones
Screenplay by: Arnold Schulman based on the stage play conceived, choreographed, and directed by Michael Bennett and written by James Kirkwood and Nicholas Dante

113 minutes; A Columbia Picture
Video distributed by: Polygram Pictures/An Embassy Home Entertainment Production

The Jewel of the Nile (1985)
Produced by: Michael Douglas
Directed by: Lewis Teague
Cast: Michael Douglas, Kathleen Turner, Danny DeVito, Avner Eisenberg, Spiros Focas, the Flying Karamazov Brothers, Holland Taylor
Screenplay by: Mark Rosenthal and Lawrence Konner based on characters created by Diane Renee Thomas
104 minutes; A 20th Century-Fox Picture
Video distributed by: CBS/Fox Video

Fatal Attraction (1987)
Produced by: Stanley R. Jaffe and Sherry Lansing
Directed by: Adrian Lyne
Cast: Michael Douglas, Glenn Close, Anne Archer
Screenplay by: James Dearden
120 minutes; A Paramount Picture

Wall Street (1987)
Produced by: Edward R. Pressman
Co-produced by: A Kitman Ho
Directed by: Oliver Stone
Cast: Michael Douglas, Charlie Sheen, Darryl Hannah, Martin Sheen, Hal Holbrook, Terence Stamp, Sean Young, Sylvia Miles
Screenplay by: Stanley Weiser and Oliver Stone
120 minutes; A 20th Century-Fox Picture

TELEVISION

(This appendix is directed at all those VCR-owning 'Streets' aficionados who are interested in collecting the episodes which co-starred Michael Douglas. Once they've been collected, it will serve as a guide.)

1. '**The Streets of San Francisco**' (two hour pilot, see Filmography).

2. '**The Thirty Years Pin**': Edmond O'Brien, Rex Holman, Tim O'Conner, Leo Gordon, Eileen Heckart, David Opatoshu. Mike Stone chases down the murderer of a friend who was due to retire after thirty years on the force. The chase scenes were shot in the tunnels being built for the future subway system.

3. '**The First Day of Forever**': Janice Rule, James Olson, Philip Pine, Joby Baker, Lawrence Montaigne, Ken Lynch. Prostitute pursued by psycho. Nice view of Fisherman's Wharf.

4. '**Forty-Five Minutes From Home**': William Windom, Robert Hogan, Jo Ann Harris, Stephen Oliver, Paul Sorensen,

John Lasell, Dick Van Patten, Jacqueline Scott. Convention delegate gets ensnared in a murder.

5. '**Whose Little Boy Are You**': James Stacy, Stephen Manley, Linda Marsh, Richard O'Brien, Nancy Wickwire. Vietnam vet abducts the son he's never seen.

6. '**Tower Beyond Tragedy**': Edward Mulhare, Sellette Cole, Stephanie Powers, Doris Dowling. An executive moulds his women into his idea of perfection and then kills them when they try to leave him. A Pygmalion who's a real pig.

7. '**Hall of Mirrors**': David Soul, Priscilla Garcia, A. Martinez, Carmen Zapata. Keller and Stone encounter problems, internal and external, while searching the big bad barrio for a Chicano youth accused of murder.

8. '**Timelock**': Peter Strauss, Bernie Casey, Elaine Giftos, Scott Walker. Mike and Steve pursue the killer who has framed a young parolee.

9. '**In the Midst of Strangers**': David Wayne, Louise Latham, Robert Foxworth, Ivan Bonar, David Pritchard, Ramon Bieri, Richard Eastham, Dennis Redfield. A mystery involving the murder of a housing commissioner, and in this case, the audience is ahead of Keller and Stone.

10. '**The Takers**': Harold Gould, Heidi Vaughn, Barbara Baxley, Michael Lerned. Two women who shared an apartment and a talent for using and abusing men run out of luck. Which one of their suckers pulled the plug?

11. '**The Year of the Locusts**': Michael Ansara, John Roper,

George Voskovec, Peggy Stanton, Christopher Stone. Gypsy con artists and an overly ambitious son-in-law whose most recent scam involves a murder.

12. '**The Bullet**': Carl Betz, Geraldine Brooks, Pat Conway, Barney Phillips. Homicide witness prefers to keep the bullet lodged in his shoulder a secret, rather than admit to his link with the killer.

13. '**Bitter Wine**': Nehemiah Persoff, Robert F. Simon, Michael Glaser, Scott Marlowe, Donna Braccala, Michael Margotta. A father won't forgive his ex-con son, who is really hiding his brother's guilt.

INDEX

INDEX